Statistical
Demography

Statistical Demography

ROLAND PRESSAT

translated and adapted
by Damien A. Courtney

ST. MARTIN'S PRESS
NEW YORK

First published in 1972 by
Presses Universitaires de France, Paris
under the title Démographie statistique
English translation first published in 1978
by Methuen & Co Ltd, London
and St. Martin's Press, Inc., New York
© 1978 Methuen & Co Ltd

Library of Congress Cataloging in Publication Data
Pressat, Roland.
    Statistical demography.

    Adapted translation of R. Pressat's Démographie statistique.
    Includes index.
    1. Demography.   2. France – – Population.
    I. Pressat, Roland.
    Démographie statistique.   II. Title.
HB881.C775   1978   301.32   78–19251
ISBN 0–312–76134–1

Contents

Translator's note

The translation and adaptation of this book involved two particular problems. One was that there is no standard translation of certain demographic terminology; in this instance the translator was helped by other works of Professor Pressat already available in English (these are referred to in the text) and by the *Multilingual Demographic Dictionary* of the United Nations. The other problem was examples from the English-speaking world; here Britain was selected from among various countries because of its similarity, demographically speaking, to France. However, British population data are not available by double classification, and moreover, satisfactory longitudinal material was difficult to obtain. Substitutions were carried out by means of *period* analysis, using British data (mostly for England and Wales; in the analysis of migration, data for the Greater London Council area and in the cartographic examples, data for Britain's sub-regions). Such adjustments were made possible by various statistical publications but especially by unpublished data from the Office of Population Censuses and Surveys in London, the whole-hearted cooperation of whose staff is gratefully acknowledged. The calculations and interpretations based on these data are of course the responsibility of the translator.

1 Population statistics

1.1 The mechanism of population change

Table 1.1 shows the sort of statistics demographers have to be familiar with. It gives the age distribution of the female population of England and Wales on 1 January[1] of two successive years (1972 and 1973). At 0 completed year of age on 1 January 1972 are all the girls born in 1971; none of them have reached their 1st birthday. At 1 completed year of age on the same date are all the girls born in 1970; they have already had their 1st birthday but not their 2nd, and so on.

The group aged 0 on 1 January 1972, totalling 369050, become those aged 1 on 1 January 1973, totalling 367200. They may be said to belong to the same *birth cohort* (or generation).[2] In the interval the totals change because of certain *vital events* (represented by the shading in Table 1.1), some of which cause a

1   Unlike in France, population estimates for England and Wales are made at mid-year, i.e. on 30 June. Thus each estimate for 1 January is simply the mean of the mid-year populations before and after, e.g.

$$P_{1.1.72} = \frac{P_{30.6.71} + P_{30.6.72}}{2}.$$

2   The two are synonymous but 'birth cohort' is more usual in English terminology.

Table. 1.1   Female population of England and Wales

Age in completed years	Population on 1 Jan. 1972	Population on 1 Jan. 1973
0	369 050	346 950
1	373 550	367 200
2	374 150	372 150
.	. .	. .
15	332 550	343 900
16	322 800	334 000
.	. .	. .
49	327 000	312 400
.	. .	. .
83	89 150	89 250
84	76 100	79 150
85 and over	232 600	331 700
Total	25 158 900	25 229 600

decrease (deaths D, departure of emigrants E), others an increase
(arrival of immigrants I). This gives us the obvious equation:

$$P_{1.1.72} - D + E - I = P_{1.1.73}. \tag{1.1}$$

Here we have an estimate only of *net emigration*[1] (emigrants
exceeding immigrants, $E - I$; otherwise it would be $I - E$, *net
immigration*). This comes to 323, and there are 1527 deaths.
So equation (1.1) now reads:

$$369050 - 1527 - 323 = 367200.$$

The cohort aged 15 completed years on 1 January 1972 suffers
116 deaths and gains 1566 from net immigration, to finish 1972
with

$$332550 - 116 + 1566 = 334000.$$

Here the gain from net immigration outweighs the loss from
deaths, and as the cohort becomes one year older it increases in
number.

This is not true of the group aged 83 on 1 January 1972; it
obviously suffers a relatively heavy loss from deaths (10015) but

---

1 These are very imprecise estimates (in England and Wales at any rate), but
this does not affect the principle of what we are doing.

is not much affected by immigration (15), since old people are far from mobile:

$$89\,150 - 10015 + 15 = 79\,150.$$

The group aged 0 on 1 January 1973, the 1972 birth cohort (or the generation born in 1972), is a special case. Its size is derived from the number of female births during 1972, which is 351 458, reduced both by deaths (3966) and estimated net emigration (542):

$$351\,458 - 3966 - 542 = 346\,950.$$

The same type of equation is used to work out the *total* female population on 1 January 1973 from that on 1 January 1972:

$$P_{1.1.72} + B - D + I - E = P_{1.1.73}.$$

Since $B = 351\,458$, and moreover $D = 291\,500$ and $I - E = 10742$,

$$25\,158\,900 + 351\,458 - 291\,500 + 10\,742 = 25\,229\,600.$$

We have just described the most obvious aspects of the mechanism of *population change* between 1 January of two successive years, and have had to consider:

the *state* of the population on two dates (1 January 1972 and 1 January 1973);
population *movement* between these dates.

We dealt very briefly with the former and merely gave its size by year of age. But the description can be extended in many ways, e.g. to take account of marital status, level of education, occupation, place of residence, nationality, etc. All these characteristics can be introduced separately or in combination.

Population movement we described in simple book-keeping terms – births, deaths, migrations – without examining the underlying mechanisms. We can again extend our analysis in many directions, e.g. in the case of births we can investigate the number of women of childbearing age, their marital status, and the number and spacing of births throughout their childbearing period.

1.2   The two types of population statistics

The two types of description and analysis we have just discussed draw on two corresponding types of demographic statistics, which depend in turn on two kinds of data collection.

As a rule the state of a population is given by a *census*, an operation generally carried out every 5 or 10 years. However, we know from our analysis of Table 1.1 that by using the initial state of a population (i.e. on 1 January 1972, derived from the 1971 census) and by examining the statistics of population movement, we can produce estimates for other dates (in our example 1 January 1973 as well). This is precisely the method employed in countries like England and Wales which publish population statistics by age and sex each year. But the census (whilst not always as accurate as we should like) provides much more extensive descriptions than can be derived from successive estimates based on the statistics of population movement, and is therefore indispensable.

The publication – sooner or later – of census results makes available a great variety of data and statistics. The total population and its geographical distribution are quickly known. To speed up the processing and publication of certain results, exhaustive collation (i.e. of all the census schedules) now regularly gives way to sampling procedures (collation of a sample of census schedules, e.g. 1 in 10, 1 in 20, etc.). And since it is impossible to publish everything that modern data-processing enables us to know, the census authorities often put together a list of statistical tables that are available on request.

Our knowledge of population movement comes from the continuous registration of *vital statistics* (births, marriages, deaths, etc.) and migrations. We shall mainly concentrate here on the *natural* movement of population, which is the result of the former events.

There is a very wide variety of sets of vital statistics; this is due not only to the mass of material about a particular *phenomenon*, such as mortality or fertility, but also to the range of associated phenomena. These annual publications are not restricted to information on the vital events (births and deaths) which directly regulate the natural movement of population; nearly all contain statistics on marriages, and many give them for divorces and remarriages; at one time particular attention was paid to the causes of death. Collation and publication are carried out in stages. The general data (number of births and deaths) are quickly known and sometimes there are adequate estimates even before the end of the particular year; they usually follow monthly or quarterly reports produced in the course of the year. But we have to wait at least a year before substantial results are published, and very often for two or three years before all statistics meant for publication have finally appeared.

We shall not deal here with statistics on *internal migration* (movement within a country) and *external migration* (change of country). They are usually second-rate because of poor recording.

1.3 Statistical publications

As well as government publications of census and vital statistics, there are many other books and periodicals we can refer to:

Statistical abstracts (annual publications of statistics, some of which relate to population).

Statistical periodicals published by official national and regional statistical organizations.

Occasional non-serial publications, sometimes published by the same organizations, on particular subjects.

Publications from other organizations which have to handle data more or less closely related to the state of the population and population change; e.g. statistics on education produced by the Department of Education and Science, on divorce by the Lord Chancellor's Department, etc.

At the international level such organizations as the United Nations, the World Health Organization, UNESCO and the O.E.C.D. devote some of their publications wholly or partly to demographic statistics; the *Demographic Yearbook* of the U.N. is particularly valuable.

1.4 Deficiencies in population statistics

The accuracy of population statistics obviously varies from one country to another. Indeed one of the analyst's preliminary tasks is to use suitable methods to correct certain deficiencies in data.

This work is always somewhat disappointing and the results will never be as good as those from data collected and handled properly.

Countries which have collected vital statistics for many years produce almost completely accurate ones. However, the census – a very big operation which must be carried out very quickly and is concerned with the state of the population at a precise date – provides statistics of much worse quality. Control checks generally reveal both omissions and double counts (at the 1961 census in England and Wales there were 1.52 omissions and 1.36 double counts per 1000). Also, some personal details will be inaccurate owing to either negligence or deception (e.g. people often conceal their divorce by declaring themselves widowed or unmarried).

A common deficiency in both census data and vital statistics is failure to supply certain information. This is shown in statistical tables by a column of 'not stated' cases (e.g. age at death not stated, family size not stated, etc.).

Of course, it is in the Third World, the developing countries, that statistical deficiencies are worst – because, among other things, of the lack of administrative machinery, individual ignorance about certain personal details (notably age) and sometimes people's more or less open hostility to some types of enquiry.

1.5   Other forms of statistical information

So far we have only dealt with traditional statistics, which are essentially administrative in origin and have a long history: the population census and the registration of births, marriages and deaths.

These sources are important but they are not the only ones. Documents from many other sources can be the starting point for demographic studies: genealogies, yearbooks of organizations, documents about life assurance and pensions, staff records, etc. (old parish registers, too, are a mine of information); all these can enhance our knowledge of the population in general, or of the mechanisms controlling the lives of particular 'populations', e.g. employees of a company, members of a professional body, etc. Since, though, these sources are not usually demographic in purpose, we shall not discuss them further.

On the other hand, existing documentation obviously cannot

satisfy all the needs of demographic research. It is, and always will be, necessary to carry out specific surveys and studies of this or that aspect of population. The variety of possible subject matter means that we cannot generalize about the form the information collected will take; though we can say that a demographic survey, which usually covers a limited number of individuals (a few thousands), is likely to produce some extremely useful information about each of them and, better still, something like their personal life history. So, whilst traditional data-collection only catches the individual at one point in time and loses sight of him thereafter (e.g. births in 1972, then those in 1973, etc.), a specific survey can often gather together many details about the *biography* of the individual. Thus the retrospective survey, by preserving the unity of the individual histories, enables us to carry out research that would be difficult or even impossible with the usual statistical information (e.g. research on the successive births of couples). Similar possibilities also arise from continuous surveys (this could be called the follow-up technique) in which a group of persons is kept under observation for a certain length of time, and from the use of suitable archive documents (e.g. the reconstruction of families by means of parish registers).

2 Population by sex and age

To understand a population we must break it down into sub-groups that are homogeneous in certain ways. We study it, therefore, by its distribution according to:

marital status;
educational status;
place of residence;
type of employment;
frequency or type of disease;
etc.

Of course, these criteria vary greatly but, whatever they may be, it is always interesting to combine them with two others that are absolutely basic, i.e. sex and age.

2.1 Sex and age in population structures

Sex and age form the basis of most types of population distribution. Why are they so privileged?

Distinction by sex is obvious, since the male and female populations have different biological, social and cultural functions and roles. Distinction by age has two reasons:

The age effect itself. Many of the individual's characteristics and aptitudes change with age (reproductive and physical ability, circumstances of employment, mental outlook, and so on).

The different eras during which comparable phases of the lives of two persons of different ages are lived. Thus in 1970, a man aged 70 had been a child and adolescent between 1900 and 1920, whereas a man aged 30 had grown up between 1940 and 1960. In a period of general social change the impression left on these two people by the environment of their formative years would most likely be different.

We single out these two factors when we distinguish between individuals by age and refer to:

the *age effect*; and
the *cohort effect*.

We use the latter term because, as we have seen, a *birth cohort* is a group of persons born during the same calendar year.

We shall see later how fruitful this distinction is.

2.2 The population pyramid

For clarity, the information in a statistical table giving population by sex and age is usually represented graphically as a population pyramid. This has the ages (birthdays) on a vertical axis and the numbers in each age group on a horizontal axis which is bisected (males on left, females on right). This is the way in which Fig. 2.1 presents some of the data from Table 2.1. It also shows the rectangle we would have drawn had we known only the total population of the group aged 50-54 completed years; this rectangle's width is determined by the average population of the five ages in question, i.e. (in 000s):

$$\frac{353.5 + 373.1 + 250.3 + 245.2 + 273.6}{5} = 299.1.$$

We have to calculate the average population when our statistics give single years of age for a particular interval (e.g. from 0 to 20 years) followed by 5- and 10-year age groups. Completing the pyramid can also be difficult, since the oldest persons in the

Table 2.1   Female population of England
and Wales on 30 June 1971 (000s)

Age in completed years	Population
0	379.3
1	368.9
.	.....
50	353.5
51	373.1
52	250.3
53	245.2
54	273.6
55	288.8
..	.....

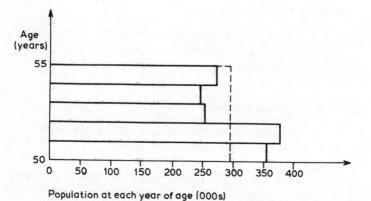

Fig. 2.1   Segments of the female population pyramid of England and
Wales on 30 June 1971

population are always grouped together. When we only know, for
example, the total of those 'aged 80 and over' (in this case,
812 600), we should distribute this population evenly over an age
range such that we exclude only a few people (this rule has to be
somewhat arbitrary). If, then, we are to distribute these 'over-80s'
over 15 years (i.e. from ages 80 to 94), we represent them by
a rectangle of width:

$$\frac{812.6}{15} = 54.2.$$

Note also that demographers sometimes mark birth cohorts on the pyramid by entering the appropriate birth dates opposite some of the rectangles; this helps comprehension and interpretation.

Now, the group aged 40 completed years on 30 June 1971 reached their 40th birthday during the preceding year; they were born, therefore, in 1970/1 − 40 = 1930/1, i.e. between mid-1930 and mid-1931.[1] In Fig. 2.2 the birth dates of 1 in 10 of the cohorts are given in this way.

How useful a population pyramid is depends on the degree of detail it shows. Figure 2.2 is excellent. We can see very clearly the double effect of age and cohort of which we just spoke: with advancing age the size of the cohort progressively diminishes (the age effect), hence the triangular shape of the pyramid; but each cohort has its own history (the cohort effect), and the various oscillations are explained by differences between cohorts in numbers born, in mortality from ordinary causes and from war, and in migration.[2]

Demographers generally complete their analysis of age structure by calculating various proportions and ratios, either to monitor particular changes or to make plain some socio-economic implications. This is why we usually determine the following distributions (the figures are for England and Wales on 30 June 1971):

Age group (years)	%	Age group (years)	%
0–19	30.53	0–14	23.71
20–59	50.31	15–64	62.94
60 and over	19.16	65 and over	13.35
	100.00		100.00

The proportion in the final group gives a measure of the relative importance of old people in the population, i.e. the *ageing of the*

1 In France, where the population is estimated on 1 January instead of on 30 June each year, those who were aged 40 completed years on 1 January 1971 can be said to belong to the 1930 birth cohort since they reached their 40th birthday during 1970, and 1970 − 40 = 1930.

2 For a further account of population pyramids see Roland Pressat, *Population* (London, Watts, 1970) pp. 21–9. This is a translation by R. and D. Atkinson of the author's *Démographie sociale* (Paris, Presses Universitaires de France, 1971).

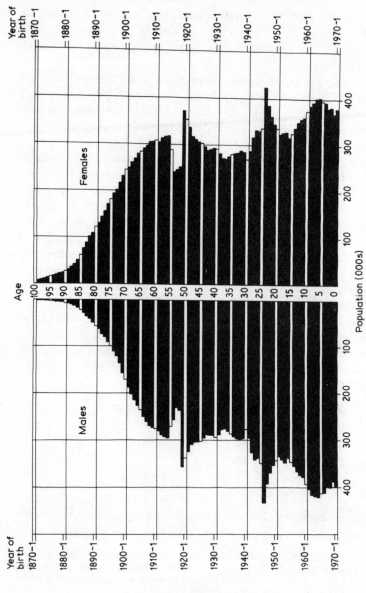

Fig. 2.2   Population pyramid of England and Wales on 30 June 1971

population. We sometimes also calculate the *average age* of the population (in England and Wales on 30 June 1971: age 37.5). Then again, certain ratios increase our awareness of the burden on a particular age group, e.g. the *dependency ratio* is sometimes calculated:

$$\frac{(0-14 \text{ years}) + (65 \text{ years and over})}{(15-64 \text{ years})} = 0.589.$$

The following ratios are very important:

$$\frac{(0-4 \text{ years})}{\text{total population}} \quad \text{and} \quad \frac{(0-4 \text{ years})}{\text{all women of childbearing age}}$$

which have to do with measuring the fertility and reproduction of a population. (We shall return to this in section 6.7.)

2.3   The sex ratio

Population pyramids are never symmetrical. This is because more boys are born than girls (the ratio is generally constant at 105%) and because mortality – the vital factor in reducing the size of cohorts – is always greater at every age in males than females. Other factors (migration, high mortality in war) can affect this 'natural' lack of balance. We move on, therefore, to the systematic study of how the proportion of males and females varies with age. We examine this by calculating the *sex ratio* (the ratio of the male to the female population) for each age. This ratio, which is 1.05 at birth, subsequently decreases if only because of normal mortality. Let us use as an example the mortality levels in England and Wales in about 1906; we find that of 10000 males born, 2990 survived to age 70, and of 10000 females born, 3765 reached 70. Since for every 10000 female births there are 10500 male births, there should for the 3765 females aged 70 be a corresponding 2990 × 1.05 = 3139 males of the same age, and accordingly a sex ratio of

$$\frac{3139}{3765} = 0.834.$$

However, at age 70 on 30 June 1971 we find that the sex ratio is 0.709.[1] This large difference is explained by the considerable fall

1 Let us clarify a small point of detail here. The first ratio (0.834) relates to the 70th birthday. The figure for 30 June 1971 relates to ages in *completed years*. Persons aged 70 completed years thus reached their 70th birthday between

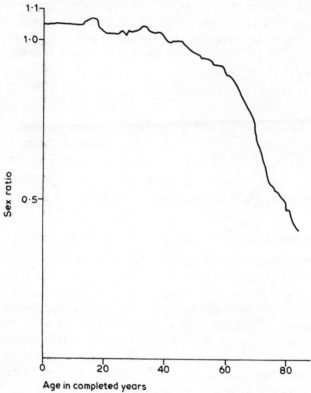

Fig. 2.3   Sex ratio by age in England and Wales on 30 June 1971

in mortality since the beginning of the century which was greater among females than males. War is another reason for higher male mortality and a lower sex ratio.

Figure 2.3 shows the variations in the sex ratio at different ages in England and Wales on 30 June 1971. Here again we can distinguish the age effect and the cohort effect, the first producing a continuous fall with age, the second a rise in the ratio during the teens (it very quickly exceeds the ratio at birth) owing to immigration, and a considerable drop after age 70 because of male losses in the First World War.

30 June 1970 and 30 June 1971; for them the sex ratio is 0.688. However, for persons who have lived 69 completed years (i.e. on average 69.5 years) the ratio is 0.73. We take the mean of these two values as an estimate of the sex ratio at *exact* age 70 on 30 June 1971.

2.4 Deficiencies in age/sex data and their correction

For various reasons population data by sex and age are often faulty:

> Over many years the census required the person's age (a changing fact) and not their birth date (an unalterable fact), so that the replies were somewhat imprecise (owing to errors in calculation by respondents who, unlike statisticians, do not always give age in completed years; they may like to give round figures, old people tend to make themselves older, and so forth).

> In much of the Third World individuals often do not know their exact birth date and, as a last resort, enumerators have to estimate age in a way that can only be approximate. People there tend to make themselves older (or sometimes younger).

> Omissions in the census are common in the Third World, particularly as regards women and young children; hence some typical variations in the sex ratio.

The statistical demographer must be able to detect these errors (or at least the most flagrant) and, if necessary, correct them in such a way as to produce results more probable than those from the raw data.

The French census of 1851, the first in France in which respondents were asked their age, provides a good example of the inaccuracy of population statistics classified by age. A segment of the female part of the pyramid (Fig. 2.4) shows the extreme irregularity in ages caused by the strong attraction of multiples of 10 (ages 30 and 40), and the smaller influence of fives and even numbers. The ratio of the number of persons at a given age, to the mean of the two adjacent ages, is sometimes suggested as an index of age regularity. Table 2.2 shows how this works out with data from the 1851 census.

With a pyramid that is regular (which is usually the case, at least for large sections) the index should never stray far from unity.[1] When it does, we try to adjust the raw data: there are

---

1 However, neither the size nor the direction of the variation from unity necessarily gives us a measure of how certain ages attract or repel. The prominence of age 32, for instance, is partly because age 30 is attractive to people aged 31. But age 32 might also have been victim to the attraction of age 30, which complicates things further....

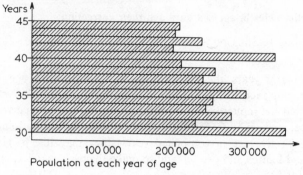

Fig. 2.4   Female population of France at the 1851 census

Table 2.2   Female population of France at the 1851 census (000s)

Age in completed years	Population (1)	Mean of adjacent ages (2)	Ratio $\dfrac{(1)}{(2)}$
27	278	—	—
28	304	260.0	1.17
29	242	328.5	0.74
30	353	234.5	1.51
31	227	315.5	0.72
32	278	234.5	1.19
33	242	—	—

various procedures which are more or less complicated but which ultimately depend on other sources of information about the particular population.

In the case of the French population in 1851, we have the size at birth of the later cohorts, and a reasonable knowledge of deaths from birth date to census date. If we use these two types of information, we can reconstruct approximately what the female population should have been on 1 May 1851 (the date of the census) without migration. We shall not, of course, replace the census data with these results but rather use them to redistribute the population enumerated in the census within carefully constituted age groups. The calculations in Table 2.3 illustrate the method; the age group has been formed symmetrically around

Table 2.3 Correction of the 1851 census results for the French female population (000s)

Age in completed years	Population enumerated (1)	Corresponding births* (2)	Probability of survival† (3)	Survivors (2) × (3) = (4)	Population in column (1) redistributed on the basis of the distribution in column (4) (5)
28	304	470.3	0.594	279.4	288
29	242	468.6	0.588	275.5	284
30	353	469.1	0.583	273.5	282
31	227	470.8	0.577	271.7	280
32	278	458.3	0.571	261.7	270
Total	1404			1361.8	1404

* Females aged 28 completed years on 1 May 1851 (date of the census), i.e. born between 1 May 1822 and 30 April 1823; 470 300 is an estimate derived from the statistics of annual births, etc.
† Taken from P. Delaporte, 'Evolution de la mortalité en Europe', *Statistique générale de la France* (Paris, 1941). The probabilities used relate to the 1820 female birth cohort.

age 30, an age which like all multiples of 10 exerts a very strong attraction. So we now have results much more likely to be accurate than the original ones, though we shall never know just how accurate they are.

When census defects (omissions, incorrect declarations of age) differ between males and females, then the sex ratio at the various ages will be distorted. This is shown in Fig. 2.5, which uses the Tunisian census of 1956; omissions of women here are flagrant since normally the sex ratio decreases with age (these omissions can, moreover, be combined with different sorts of inaccurate age declaration). One way to correct such data is to select a credible series of sex ratios and apply them to the male population, which is assumed to have been correctly registered (its age distribution can be amended first). This was done for the Tunisian population – the sex ratios selected to correct the female population were probably based on comparison of carefully chosen male and female life tables (see Table 2.4 and Fig. 2.5). This type of calculation presupposes that male migration is not too important or, at any rate, that migration affects each sex similarly.

Then again, there are the typical curves of sex ratios at different ages in French-speaking black African countries. The similarity of these curves justifies our drawing a single one for all their populations (see Fig. 2.6). The extremely low sex ratio at ages

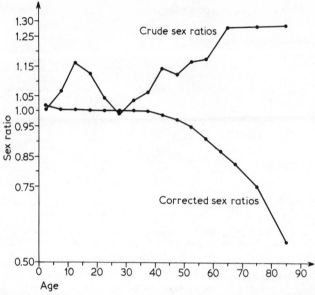

Fig. 2.5   Population of Tunisia at the 1956 census: crude and corrected sex ratios

Table 2.4   Muslim population of Tunisia at the census of 1 February 1956 (000s)

Age group (years)	Population enumerated			Corrected male population* (4)	Corrected sex ratio (5)	Corrected female population (6) = $\frac{(4)}{(5)}$
	Males (1)	Females (2)	Sex ratio (3) = $\frac{(1)}{(2)}$			
0–4	308810	306200	1.009	302800	1.020	296900
5–9	251700	236100	1.066	246400	1.009	244300
10–14	184570	159950	1.154	193600	1.006	192500
15–19	163810	145120	1.129	165500	1.006	164500
20–24	150680	144100	1.046	147000	1.003	146500
25–29	136430	136970	0.996	129600	1.004	129100
...	...	...	...	...	...	...
60–69	59860	47060	1.272	62300	0.851	73200
70–79	30760	24030	1.280	30400	0.752	40400
80 and over	9690	7540	1.285	10700	0.569	18800
Total	1758280	1625630		1758300		1785700

* i.e. the age distribution has been corrected.

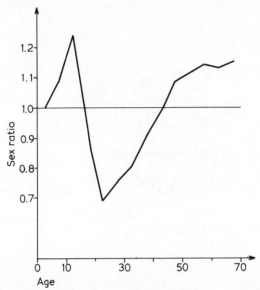

Fig. 2.6 Variations in the sex ratio by age in the French-speaking populations of Black Africa and in Madagascar

Source: F. Gendreau and R. Nadot, 'Structures par âge, actuelle et future (Afrique noire, Madagascar, Comores)', *Démographie comparée*, Paris, 1967.

15–30 is the result of an ageing process imposed on young women by the enumerators:

> Around age 15 a woman is systematically assumed to be older if she is married, since the interviewers consider that a married woman is automatically over 15. Likewise, the married woman who has the most children is considered even older, though in fact she is still young (Gendreau and Nadot, op. cit.).

However, the correction of such data involves the use of more refined techniques and, in particular, of stable population models.

3 The analysis of population structures

3.1 Population by marital status

We have seen that a preliminary breakdown by age and sex is the foundation of all further demographic analysis. Table 3.1, accordingly, examines marital status by sex (in this case female) and by age; for purposes of analysis the population is distributed on a base of 1000[1] on the right-hand side.

We can clearly see how the distributions by marital status change continuously with age. Early marriages reduce the proportion of single persons and increase the proportion of married ones. Then, since chances of survival diminish gradually with age, the proportion of widows increases at the expense of the married. The proportion divorced undergoes more irregular changes, particularly because the cohort effect is more important here. The possibility of widows or the divorced remarrying is much less significant.

We must pay special attention to the series of the *proportion single* (column 6 of Table 3.1). As we shall learn, in order to

---

1 And not for each type of marital status as sometimes happens. Nor is the *total* population reduced to a multiple of 10.

describe and analyse different population structures by sex and age, we calculate the proportion of the population in a particular category (single persons, the labour force, schoolchildren and students, etc.) at each age (or age group).

The proportion single is an almost perfect gauge of both the timing and extent of marriages among them (the *nuptiality* of single persons): the more single persons marry before a given age, the smaller the proportion single. The following data show a variety of situations:

Proportion single (%)

	Males		Females	
	20–24 years	*45–49 years*	*20–24 years*	*45–49 years*
England and Wales (1951)	76	10	52	15
United States (1950)	59	9	32	8
France (1954)	82	11	57	10
Algeria (Moslems) (1958)	68	5	23	2
Korea (1930)	33	1	2	0

We shall return to this index when we study nuptiality. However, before we leave Table 3.1, we should note the increase in the proportion single after ages 35–39, an increase inconceivable within a particular cohort. This clearly reveals the cohort effect: the frequency of first marriages tends to increase with more recent cohorts.

3.2 Other types of structure

The data and calculations in Table 3.2 illustrate two other kinds of proportion: the *proportion of labour force participation* and the *proportion in full-time education*, which are the proportions of the economically active population and of schoolchildren and students, respectively, of a given age or age group, in the total population of this age or age group. Properly speaking, they are not demographic characteristics but exactly the same type of analysis is applicable. Note that in this case a person can leave and later rejoin the labour force (so returning to a former condition; something that single persons cannot do), and that we all

Table 3.1 Estimated female population of England and Wales by age and marital status on 30 June 1971 (000s)

Age in completed years	Female population					Proportion per 1000 women at each age			
	Total (1)	Single (2)	Married (3)	Widowed (4)	Divorced (5)	Single (6) = $\frac{(2)}{(1)}$	Married (7) = $\frac{(3)}{(1)}$	Widowed (8) = $\frac{(4)}{(1)}$	Divorced (9) = $\frac{(5)}{(1)}$
0–4	1901.9	1901.9	—	—	—	—	—	—	—
5–9	1974.0	1974.0	—	—	—	—	—	—	—
10–14	1771.1	1771.1	—	—	—	—	—	—	—
15	326.4	326.4	—	—	—	—	—	—	—
16	317.2	313.5	3.7	—	—	988	12	—	—
17	327.6	311.5	16.1	—	—	951	49	—	—
18	326.8	284.2	42.6	—	—	870	130	—	—
19	323.2	244.8	78.2	0.1	0.1	758	242	—	—
15–19	**1621.2**	**1480.4**	**140.6**	**0.1**	**0.1**	**913**	**87**	—	—
20	334.6	212.1	122.1	0.1	0.2	634	365	—	1
21	346.3	175.2	170.2	0.2	0.7	506	491	1	2
22	360.5	139.6	219.1	0.3	1.5	387	608	1	4
23	384.9	112.5	269.3	0.4	2.7	292	700	1	7
24	423.8	95.0	324.1	0.6	4.1	224	765	1	10

	1850.1	734.3	1104.9	1.6	9.2	397	597	1	5
20–24									
25	336.0	60.8	270.0	0.6	4.6	181	803	2	14
26	329.2	48.3	275.2	0.6	5.1	147	836	2	15
27	332.2	41.4	283.8	0.9	6.1	125	854	3	18
28	316.5	34.4	274.9	0.9	6.3	109	868	3	20
29	286.8	27.9	251.8	1.0	6.1	97	878	4	21
25–29	**1600.7**	**212.8**	**1355.7**	**4.0**	**28.2**	**133**	**847**	**2**	**18**
30–34	1410.8	110.6	1259.0	7.7	33.5	78	892	6	24
35–39	1378.1	97.1	1233.1	15.3	32.6	70	895	11	24
40–44	1463.9	108.6	1289.3	32.7	33.3	74	881	22	23
45–49	1575.7	123.3	1348.3	67.9	36.2	78	856	43	23
50–54	1495.7	124.5	1219.1	119.0	33.1	83	815	80	22
55–59	1540.9	147.6	1150.5	212.5	30.3	96	746	138	20
60–64	1511.7	173.5	982.5	330.6	25.1	115	650	219	16
65–69	1341.9	177.8	705.4	442.0	16.7	133	526	329	12
70–74	1089.9	151.3	420.3	509.3	9.0	139	386	467	8
75 and over	1591.2	244.4	299.6	1041.0	6.2	154	188	654	4

Table 3.2   Female population of England and Wales at the 1971 census

Age*	Total population (1)	Labour force (2)	Proportion of labour participation per 1000 $(3) = \frac{(2)}{(1)}$	Students (4)	Proportion in full-time education per 1000 $(5) = \frac{(4)}{(1)}$
15	331584	29968	90	287975	868
16	322948	109066	338	201964	625
17	321084	171717	535	138242	431
18	325043	213434	657	89812	276
19	323640	223609	691	62025	192
15–19	1624299	747794	460	780018	480
20	327716	223195	681	47269	144
21–24	1364627	745378	546	394925	289
20–24	1692343	968573	572	442194	261
25–29	1768168	981227	555	78236	44
30–44	4331702	2139619	494	26506	6
45–64	6092708	3393288	557	8967	1
65 and over	5038728	547799	109	—	—

* Birthday reached during 1971 (see explanations in section 3.4).

revert at some stage to being outside full-time education, each cohort having started by being outside it. . . .

We have recognized two factors – the age effect and the cohort effect – as causing changes in the proportions of a population distributed by age. However, when we examine the results of just one census, we cannot generally distinguish the part played by each of them. We must, therefore, be particularly careful not to interpret a series of such proportions at a given moment (e.g. columns 3 and 5 of Table 3.2) as the result merely of people getting older.

We can calculate many other proportions based on classifying a population into two categories. We can take place of residence (urban or rural), occupation (agricultural or non-agricultural), educational status (distinguishing perhaps between those who stayed at school after 16 and those who did not) and the innumerable physical, physiological and behavioural characteristics of individuals. Importantly, we can work out by age and sex the frequency with which people suffer a particular illness or disease, such as tuberculosis or cancer. Epidemiologists refer to the frequency of a disease as its *prevalence*.

Individuals may, of course, be differentiated not only by 'dichotomy' but also by sliding scales that measure very diverse

Table 3.3 Live births in Great Britain to marriages concluded by single women before reaching age 45, and surviving in January and February 1946 (births before marriage included)

Marriage duration* (years)	Number of women	Number of live births											Average number per woman	No births (%)
		0	1	2	3	4	5	6	7	8	9	10 and over		
1	23554	20455	2866	173	32	10	6	7	4			1	0.15	86.8
2	23834	13517	9645	601	51	10	3	3	2	1		1	0.47	56.7
3	24400	10729	11614	1889	138	18	6	2	1	1		3	0.65	44.0
4	31504	12621	14248	4120	443	53	8	4	4		1	2	0.77	40.1
5	32653	11120	14526	5849	1013	121	14	5	1		1	3	0.92	34.1
...	...	...	...	...	...	...	...	...	...	...	...	...	...	...
25	24401	3544	5517	5976	3757	2203	1277	802	505	324	181	315	2.46	14.5

* Calculated as the calendar year difference between the year of the census (1946) and the year of the marriage.
Source: D. V. Glass and E. Grebenik, *The Trend and Pattern of Fertility in Great Britain* (London, 1954).

Table 3.4 Daily consumption of cigarettes by age among the male population of the U.S.A. in 1966

Age group (years)	Population surveyed	Daily consumption of cigarettes							Average consumption	Non-smokers (%)
		0	Less than 1*	1 to 9	10 to 20	21 to 40	41 and over	Unknown		
18–24	8828	4325	0	549	2839	521	58	241	7.47	50.4
25–34	10231	4006	43	450	£784	1450	125	194	10.82	39.9
35–44	11306	4574	49	504	3627	1818	213	288	11.03	41.5
45–54	10595	4703	36	449	3164	1506	170	269	9.97	45.5
55–64	8093	4011	26	433	2055	929	82	345	8.50	52.4
65 and over	7717	5570	29	430	1089	227	0	245	3.44	74.5

* In the original document this column represents the 'occasional smokers'.
Source: Changes in Cigarette Smoking Habits between 1955 and 1966, National Centre for Health Statistics, April 1970, ser. 10, no. 59.

characteristics. We can also adopt a time scale other than age, e.g. marriage duration, in censuses and in surveys of the number of children born.

Tables 3.3 and 3.4 give two very different examples of population structure, from which we can for instance extract: the distribution of certain married women in Great Britain by year of marriage and number of live births; and a distribution of men in the U.S.A. by age group and daily consumption of cigarettes.

In such cases it is interesting to summarize the distribution of individuals on the chosen scale, by giving the average value of the distribution,[1] as well as to determine the number of persons not involved in the phenomenon, e.g. to calculate the proportion of women who have had no live births (the proportion infertile) or of non-smoking men, or the complementary proportions. The average values should be analysed with the same care as the proportions themselves.

Preparing these summary indexes obviously does not reduce the interest of studying the distribution of individuals by age and characteristics.

3.3   Comparison of successive censuses

To compare data on successive states of the same population is generally most rewarding, especially when one can monitor changes affecting the *same groups of cohorts*. For one to be able to do this, the number of years between censuses or surveys must correspond to the number of years in the age groups under consideration.[2]

One of the best examples is provided by the series of French censuses carried out every five years up to the last war (from 1851 with the exception of 1872 and a gap in 1916), which give certain characteristics (including marital status) by corresponding five-year age groups. Part of the series, providing this type of

1 Because of the very wide consumption classes in Table 3.4, the calculation of average consumption is very imprecise. It neglects the occasional smokers and adopts 6, 15, 30 and 45 as the average consumption classes.
2 Strictly speaking, it is sufficient that the intercensal period be a multiple of the number of years composing the age groups. Thus, with a breakdown by single year of age and a census every five years, we can follow each cohort (albeit imperfectly); and with a constant breakdown into five-year age groups and a census every ten years, we can follow each group of five cohorts.

Table 3.5   Percentage single in France (females)

Age group (years)	Censuses							
	1876	*1881*	*1886*	*1891*	*1896*	*1901*	*1906*	*1911*
15–19	93.7	93.9	94.4	95.3	95.5	93.5	93.6	92.3
20–24	56.8	60.2	61.0	61.9	62.9	58.2	(54.0)	54.0
25–29	29.1	31.9	*32.7*	32.0	31.2	29.5	(29.0)	26.4
30–34	19.9	22.4	23.1	*21.5*	20.7	18.6	(17.9)	17.4
35–39	15.5	17.6	18.3	17.1	*16.4*	14.5	(15.0)	14.0
40–44	13.3	15.3	15.9	15.0	14.5	*12.7*	(12.5)	12.6
45–49	11.8	13.3	14.5	13.5	13.2	11.6	(*11.6*)	11.3

Note: the figures for 1906, in brackets, are estimates from data based on 10-year age groups.

Table 3.6   Average number of cigarettes consumed daily and percentage of non-smokers in the U.S.A. (males)

Age group (years)	Average number of cigarettes consumed daily		Percentage of non-smokers	
	1955	*1966*	*1955*	*1966*
18–24	7.86	7.47	43.4	50.4
25–34	11.31	10.82	32.6	39.9
35–44	11.66	11.03	34.0	41.5
45–54	10.48	9.97	38.6	45.5
55–64	7.44	8.50	51.6	52.4
65 and over	3.21	3.44	73.2	74.5

information, appears in Table 3.5. The history of several groups of cohorts can easily be followed from beginning to end: *italics* are used to indicate the group aged 15–19 at the 1876 census. Since the census took place early in the year (in March) we can assimilate this group to that of the same age (in completed years) on 1 January 1876 without serious inaccuracy. We are concerned, therefore, with persons who reached their 15–19th birthdays during 1875, i.e. those born between 1875 − 19 = 1856, and 1875 − 15 = 1860. As we have seen, these proportions single are a fundamental indicator of both the timing and extent of first marriages in the relevant groups of cohorts.

Let us now return to some of the data in Table 3.4 (for 1966).

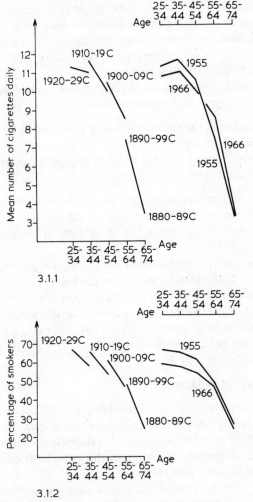

Fig. 3.1   U.S.A. (males): 3.1.1 average number of cigarettes consumed daily; and 3.1.2 percentage of smokers by age (C = birth cohorts)

Equivalent measures can be calculated for the same age groups in 1955 (see Table 3.6). Here, the period between the two surveys (11 years) is a little greater than the composition of the age groups between ages 25 and 65 (10 years). If we accept that this slight time displacement does not prevent our attributing the 1955 data for a certain age group and the 1966 data for an age group 10 years older to the same group of cohorts; and if again we assimilate to the 65–74 age group the data for the group aged 65 and over, we can produce the graphs shown in Fig. 3.1. (Fig. 3.1.2 gives percentages not of non-smokers but of smokers, so as to be compatible with 3.1.1.)

Each type of information can be presented in two ways depending on the aspect of the phenomenon we wish to illustrate:

by separating the data for different years (as on the right-hand side of Fig. 3.1);

by separating the data for different groups of cohorts (as on the left-hand side).

The first, in some ways more literal, enables us to stress changes in the phenomenon at different ages: a fall in consumption up to age 55, then a rise, but a fall at all ages in the proportion of smokers.

The second isolates the behaviour of different groups of cohorts. It gives a longitudinal view of the phenomenon, which is particularly expressive in Fig. 3.1.2 where a concerted tendency is very clear: all the cohorts are engaged in a downward movement which allows us to predict, if the trend continues, a considerable drop in the percentage of smokers.

3.4 Ways of defining 'age'

In most instances we have considered a population classified by age on 30 June (see p. 1, fn 1). In France, however, the population is estimated on 1 January, which is extremely convenient since on this date all persons belonging to the same birth cohort are the same age in *completed years*.

Thus, persons born in 1929 have their 41st birthday in 1970 (1929+41 = 1970), and on 1 January 1971 (at midnight on 31 December 1970 to be precise) none of them have yet reached their 42nd birthday; on this date they are the group aged 41 completed years.

A simple form of illustration (the Lexis diagram, Fig. 3.2) demonstrates this. Dates are placed on a horizontal axis and birthdays on a vertical axis. Persons born in 1929 appear on the corresponding segment (*ca*) of the horizontal axis and, as time passes, move up the ascending corridor, enclosed by the two

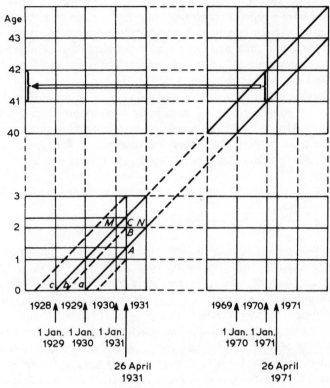

Fig. 3.2   Lexis diagram

heavy diagonals, at an angle of 45°. On 1 January 1971 these persons (or rather the survivors) are marked by a bracket on a vertical segment; on the vertical axis there is a corresponding place for all the exact ages between 41 and 42, i.e. the whole group aged 41 completed years. At a date other than 1 January, say 26 April or even 30 June, there would be no such correspondence.

Let us analyse what actually happens on 26 April 1931 (the census of England and Wales has nearly always taken place in April), again using the 1929 birth cohort. On this date the larger segment of the cohort (*AB*) is still aged 1 completed year, whilst the smaller segment (*BC*) is already aged 2 completed years, the former having been born on *ab* (i.e. from 26 April to 31 December 1929), and the latter on *bc* (1 January to 25 April 1929).

A classification by age on 26 April 1931, or indeed on 30 June, would have resulted in a *blending of cohorts*, since on either date the group aged 1 completed year comprised certain new-borns of both 1930 and 1929, and those aged 2 completed years comprised certain new-borns of both 1929 and 1928 (as indicated by the broken diagonal lines in Fig. 3.2).

Because a cohort is what it is, we do not often proceed in this way: we usually resort to classification by cohort or group of cohorts. However, ages *do* appear in statistical tables, so we must understand properly how they are designated. Thus, referring again to the 1929 cohort, on 26 April 1931 we record:

age 1 if the column heading specifies age in completed years on 1 January 1931;

age 2 if it specifies age reached during 1931.

The 1929 cohort does in fact cross the segment *MN*, corresponding to the 2nd birthday, during 1931. Here we refer to *age by calendar year difference*, because it is by taking the difference between year of observation (1931) and year of birth (1929) that we obtain the age reached during 1931. This latter mode of description was used in Table 3.2, which contains results from the census of 26 April 1971. Thus, the 322 948 females it describes as aged 16 will reach (or have already reached) this age during 1971. If we had wished to give their age in completed years on 1 January 1971 we would have put age 15.

Similarly, Table 3.3 gives marriage duration by *calendar year difference*, i.e. the 4-year duration calculated in January–February 1946 (survey date) refers to the marriages of 1942 (1946 − 1942 = 4). In other words, the exact 4-year duration will only be reached on the actual anniversary date in 1946.

3.5 Families and households

We now move on to population structures based on completely different groupings, i.e. families or households. These everyday terms cause all sorts of confusion when they are not used according to precise demographic definitions. Our definitions here will refer, more or less explicitly, to British statistics.

The *family* generally consists of father, mother and children.

Table 3.7 Lone female parents by age and number of dependent children in Great Britain at the 1971 census (1% sample)

Dependent children in family	Lone female parent aged				
	All ages	*Under 30*	*30–44*	*45–59*	*60 and over*
0*	6079	—	244	1 864	3 971
1	2613	693	862	907	151
2	1408	397	713	280	18
3	601	168	350	80	3
4	234	45	160	26	3
5 or more	142	23	106	13	—
Total	11077	1 326	2 435	3 170	4 146

* i.e. the children are no longer dependent.
Source: Census 1971, Great Britain, *Summary Tables* (*1% sample*) (London, H.M.S.O., 1973).

We sometimes speak of either the *primary* or the *nuclear family*[1] as opposed to the *extended family*, which takes in a wider range of relatives.

A family, thus defined, need not have all these components in order to remain a family; a family can be

a couple without children;
a widow or widower with or without children.

A divorce should as a rule result in two families:

that of one spouse, and the children he or she is looking after;
that of the other spouse.

However, statistics about families never include the total number of children; there is always an age limit, e.g. children under 18, under 16, etc.

If we combine such data with the age of the head of the family, we obtain summary statistics of family dependency; the data do not provide statistics of fertility. Table 3.7 is an example from the 1971 British census.

Until recently French statistics included something called '*Statistique des familles*' (fertility of marriages), which had a com-

---

1 In French terminology this is referred to as the *biological family*. However, since 1962, only unmarried children under 25 have been included in French statistics.

pletely different meaning. This comprised *all* a couple's children who were *born alive*, classified according to the mother's age, regardless of whether they survived until the census date. These were fertility statistics similar to those for Great Britain used in Table 3.3.

The *household* is a group of persons living in the same dwelling. This is usually an ordinary house or flat but it can be an independent room, e.g. a hotel room, a bedsitter, etc. The household may be broken down into its components, so that we can have:

> *no family* households, consisting either of one person or two or more persons who may or may not be related;
>
> *one family* households, consisting of married couples or lone parents, with child(ren) or others, or both, or just alone;
>
> *two, three* or more *family households*, either of direct descent or not. It is interesting to note that 'In households consisting of more than one family, any two families were described as "two families, direct descent", if one family contained a descendant (i.e. child, grandchild or great grandchild by blood, adoption or marriage) of a member of the other family. This ancestor descendant link could span more than one generation, and other families or individuals could lie on the line of descent between the two families so linked' (Census 1971, op. cit. in Table 3.7, p. xxi).

Table 3.8 shows how the 181 874 households (1% sample) enumerated in the 1971 British census were distributed.

We can, for households, calculate proportions like those we have already come across, e.g. the *proportion of household heads* by sex, age and marital status. Using the 1971 census again, the proportion of married men aged under 30 who are heads of households is:

$$\frac{1\,983\,600}{2\,082\,800} = 0.952,$$

and the proportion of lone female parents aged 45–49 who are heads of households is:

$$\frac{317\,000}{558\,400} = 0.568.[1]$$

---

[1] This index is under-estimated as the denominator includes all widows and divorcees, some of whom were never parents.

Table 3.8 Households by type and size in Great Britain at the 1971 census (1% sample)

Household types	Persons in household										Total households	Total persons	Persons per household
	1	2	3	4	5	6	7	8	9	10+			
No family	32 553	6 114	939	215	80	28	6	2	2	—	39 939	49 102	1.23
One family	—	50 928	33 674	30 621	14 379	5 932	2 219	935	420	286	139 394	462 716	3.32
Two families	—	—	—	668	742	509	267	141	75	97	2 499	14 178	5.67
Three or more families	—	—	—	—	—	4	6	7	6	19	42	402	9.57
All household types	32 553	57 042	34 613	31 504	15 201	6 473	2 498	1 085	503	402	181 874	526 398	2.89

Source: Census 1971, Great Britain, Summary Tables (1% sample) (London, H.M.S.O., 1973).

These proportions are particularly interesting because they enable us to establish projections of the numbers of households; in so far as such proportions are extrapolated into the future, we need only apply them to the corresponding population projections by sex, age and marital status, to work out the resulting number of future households.

4 Mortality

With mortality, we come to the demographic phenomena (mortality, nuptiality, fertility, divorce, etc.) characterized by *vital events* (deaths, marriages, births, divorces, etc.) of which the demographer generally takes stock each year.

The *crude death rate* (or simply, the death rate) is the first measure of mortality. It is the ratio of the number of deaths during a given year to the *mean population* of that year; the mean population is that on 30 June, the mid-point of the year (or if the population is estimated on 1 January, as in France, the mean population is the mean of the populations on the previous and the subsequent 1 January), and is an estimate of the number of persons exposed, during a whole year, to the risk of dying (the mean population is, in this sense, a sum of *person-years*, an idea we shall return to).

England and Wales had a population of 48 933 900 on 30 June 1971. We relate to this the 567 262 deaths recorded during the year, and arrive at a death rate of

$$\frac{567\,262}{48\,933\,900} = 11.6 \text{ per 1000 persons.}$$

We must emphasize the annual dimension of such rates. Thus, in order to calculate the death rate for the period 1971–2 we relate the mean of the deaths of the years in question,

$$\frac{567\,262 + 591\,889}{2} = 579\,576,$$

to the population at the mid-point of the period (in this instance, 1 January 1972, therefore the mean of the populations on 30 June 1971 and 1972):

$$\frac{48\,933\,900+49\,110\,500}{2} = 49\,022\,200.$$

We obtain:

$$\frac{579\,576}{49\,022\,200} = 11.8 \text{ per 1000 persons.}$$

On the other hand, if we wish to calculate the death rate just for September 1971, we must take the *average daily number* of deaths during that September, multiply it by 365 (days in the year) and divide the result by 30 (days in the month):

$$\frac{41\,091 \times 365}{30} = 499\,941,$$

and relate this total to the estimated population for mid-September.

4.1   Mortality by age and sex

Obviously, mortality in individuals varies considerably with age; hence the idea of calculating rates by age. Each sex is usually treated separately because of the differences between male and female mortality.

The principle behind the calculation of death rates by age and sex (hereafter referred to as age-sex-specific mortality rates) is the same as for a crude rate: the ratio of the number of deaths occurring to persons of a certain age during a given year, to the mean population of that age in the same year. However, there can be specific difficulties about collecting the statistical data required.

Normally we have at our disposal the number of deaths by age in completed years for the particular year, in this case 1971, and the population by age in completed years on 30 June, the mid-point of the year (see Table 4.1). This table gives an idea of how the risk of death changes with advancing age. Figure 4.1 gives a more complete view: a diminishing risk up to age 12, then a mostly uninterrupted increase, with excess male mortality at every age.

Table 4.1   Age-sex-specific mortality rates for
England and Wales, 1971

Age in completed years	Deaths	Mid-year population	Rates per 1000
Males			
5	214	415400	0.5
10	137	395100	0.3
20	344	345100	1.0
30	273	278700	1.0
40	678	295000	2.3
60	5766	276800	20.8
80	7262	58000	125.2
Females			
5	137	394700	0.3
10	97	373400	0.3
20	146	334600	0.4
30	159	268600	0.6
40	492	292200	1.7
60	3125	308700	10.1
80	9934	122000	81.4

To describe mortality age by age, we need to calculate about
100 male and 100 female rates, since human life hardly ever
exceeds 100 years. But it is often sufficient to confine ourselves to
about 20 5-year rates for each sex, particularly as annual rates[1]
for ages at low risk, even with totals as large as those of the
cohorts of England and Wales, are affected by short-term variations which take away much of their significance. The method
being the same throughout, let us calculate the rate just for the
female age group 40–44.

Deaths	*Average population*	*Rate per 1000*
2943	1463900	2.0

1 Here and elsewhere, unless otherwise stated, annual rates signify rates
   referring to a whole year of age, it being understood that the observation
   period is one calendar year or its equivalent.

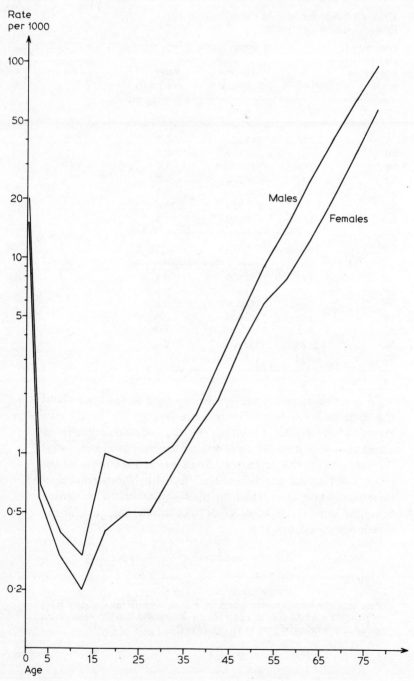

Fig. 4.1   Age-sex-specific mortality rates for England and Wales in 1971

Here the 5-year rate is of the same order of magnitude as the annual rate for the adjoining ages (1.7 per 1000 at age 40, see Table 4.1). However, we shall see later that annual and 5-year probabilities of death differ radically.

4.2 Double classification of deaths

There is a type of death classification more elaborate than that in Table 4.1, i.e. by age and by cohort (or year of birth), called *double classification*. Unfortunately it is not possible when we use British population data.

To understand the principle behind it, let us employ French statistics and consider the deaths among males aged 40 in France in 1961; they total 1264. This number can, however, be split in two according to the year of birth of the deceased (i.e. their birth cohort). A person can die at 40 completed years of age in 1961,

having been born in $1961 - 40 = 1921$, if 1961 is the year of his 40th birthday;

having been born in $1961 - 41 = 1920$, if 1961 is the year of his 41st birthday.

In the former case, deaths during the calendar year occur *after* the birthday (the 40th), in the latter *before* the birthday (which would have been the 41st) (see Fig. 4.2).

Countries which publish their statistics of death (and of some other demographic events) by double classification are becoming more and more numerous; in France, for example, statistics of deaths around age 40 in 1961 are given the following form:

Year of birth	Age in completed years	Males		
1922	38		465	
1922	39		552	
1921	39		538	1171
1921	40	1264	633	
1920	40		631	
1920	41		744	
1919	41		459	

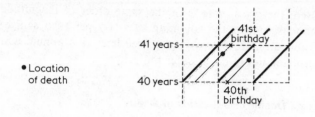

• Location
of death

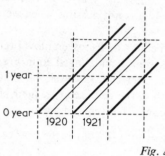

Fig. 4.2

Thus, the 1264 deaths of persons aged 40 completed years are divided between 633 deaths from the 1921 cohort and 631 from the 1920 cohort.

Double classification of deaths is extremely useful in the direct calculation of *probabilities of dying*, a basic index for constructing *life tables*, to which we shall return later. Also, double classification allows us to calculate a different sort of rate from the one we have just discussed: instead of regrouping the deaths by completed years of age, we regroup them by year of birth, i.e. by cohort. Thus, among the 1921 cohort,

$$538 + 633 = 1171 \text{ deaths}$$

occur during 1961. The size of this cohort was

336700 (aged 39 completed years) on 1 January 1961,
336500 (aged 40 completed years) on 1 January 1962;[1]

so that its mean population during 1961 was:

$$\frac{336700 + 336500}{2} = 336600.$$

---

1 The cohort has only decreased by 200 persons (round figures), although nearly 1200 have died; the difference is due to net immigration.

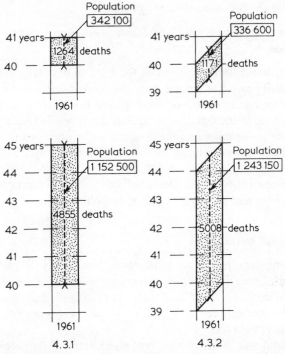

Fig. 4.3   Methods of calculating death rates at ages 40 and 40–44 for French males: 4.3.1 period rates; 4.3.2 cohort rates

Therefore the death rate for the 1921 *cohort* during 1961 was:

$$\frac{1171}{336\,600} = 3.5 \text{ per } 1000.$$

This is called a *cohort rate* (or generation rate) and is the mortality rate of persons who reached (or would have reached) age 40 during 1961. Their deaths occurred in that calendar year between their 39th and 41st birthdays, i.e. *on average* at exact age 40, whereas the rate for those aged 40 completed years relates to persons of average age 40.5 (it is interesting that the first rate is slightly lower than the second: 3.5 per 1000 instead of 3.7).

Similarly, as well as the rate for those aged 40–44 completed years, we can determine the rate for the group of cohorts reaching ages 40–44 during 1961, i.e. the group of 1917–21 birth cohorts.

We have the following data for this group:

Deaths	Average population	Rate per 1000
5008	1 243 150	4.0

The previous rate was calculated for a group of average age 42.5 completed years (see section 4.1); the present one is for a group of average age 42 (this time displacement is shown by the rate of 4.2 per 1000 in the first case as against 4.0 here). Figure 4.3 illustrates these examples and the distinctions between them.

Similar distinctions can be made in fertility and nuptiality rates.

In France, I.N.S.E.E. (National Institute of Statistics) gives *cohort* rates and not *period* rates in its publications.

4.3 Infant mortality

Demographers pay special attention, and apply a particular method of analysis, to *infant mortality*, which is the mortality of children under 1 year of age. Sex is not usually distinguished since the difference between male and female mortality does not in this case perceptibly change.

England and Wales can provide an example of the calculation of a traditionally defined *infant mortality rate*:

Deaths at 0 completed year of age in 1971   13 720

Live births in 1971   783 155

Infant mortality rate $= \dfrac{13\,720}{783\,155} = 17.5$ per 1000 live births.

It is interesting to note, however, that in France the calculation of the infant mortality rate, based on similar data, must be adjusted if the rate is to be compared with that of other countries. This is because only the infants still alive at the time of registration appear in the vital statistics as live births, even though registration may take place up to three days after birth. Infants born alive, but who die before registration, thus escape both the death and the live-birth statistics. We call this event *erroneous stillbirth*. It is estimated that there were 3393 such in France in 1961; if this is taken into account, the 1961 infant mortality rate changes from 21.7 to 25.6 per 1000 live births. We obtain the revised figure by adding the number of erroneous stillbirths to both numerator and denominator:

$$\frac{18\,100+3393}{835\,240+3393} = 25.6 \text{ per 1000.}$$

To conclude this analysis of infant mortality, we should mention certain terms and indexes associated with death around the time of birth.

The frequency of (true) stillbirths is usually measured by relating them to the number of live births. In England and Wales in 1971, there were 9899 stillbirths and 783 155 live births. These give a *stillbirth rate* of

$$\frac{9899}{783\,155} = 12.6 \text{ per 1000 live births.}$$

Neonatal mortality occurs during the first four weeks or 30 days of life, and the *neonatal mortality rate* is determined by relating these deaths to live births, as in England and Wales in 1971:

$$\frac{9113}{783\,155} = 11.6 \text{ per 1000 live births.}$$

The *perinatal mortality rate* is determined by adding the stillbirth rate to the neonatal mortality rate. Thus, the perinatal mortality rate of England and Wales in 1971 was:

$$12.6+11.6 = 24.2 \text{ per 1000 live births.}$$

This merging of stillbirths with neonatal deaths is justified by the similarity of their causes, which are sometimes termed *endogenous*. There are simple methods for separating endogenous and *exogenous* deaths among all deaths under age 1, but we shall not examine them in this book.

4.4   Different ways of calculating the infant mortality rate

We calculate the infant mortality rate in order to measure the *proportion* of new-borns who die before age 1. An accurate way of doing this, on the basis of the 783 155 new-borns of 1971, is to add together the deaths under age 1 in this birth cohort (deaths in both 1971 and 1972) and to relate them to the births. With 13 109 deaths under age 1,[1] the *cohort infant mortality rate* is:

$$\frac{13\,109}{783\,155} = 16.7 \text{ per 1000 live births.}$$

This differs from the rate previously given (17.5 per 1000) since it reflects the mortality level in both 1971 and 1972, the two operative years. This sort of infant mortality rate is the same as the *probability of dying* (at age 0); we have already mentioned the latter and shall discuss it fully later on.

However, it is useful in practice to have measures of mortality for single calendar years, in order to follow short-term variations accurately and to relate them to changes in different factors (e.g. climatic or epidemiological). If the traditional method of calculation is not entirely satisfactory, it is because it does not relate the infant deaths to all the new-borns at risk of dying during the year, since those who are under age 1 when they die in 1972 can have been born in either 1972 or 1971. To take this into account, and so improve the calculation of the rate for a single year, deaths under age 1 are related to a *weighted mean of births* for that year and the previous one (however, this sort of refinement only makes sense if the number of births differs considerably between the two years). The choice of the weighting factor, which takes into account the relative influence of the two cohorts of new-borns on the deaths of the particular year, depends on the level of infant mortality; an approximate choice is adequate here. These generalizations are illustrated in the (fictitious) calculations of Table 4.2, where the weight of births for the year is in inverse proportion to the level of infant mortality. And we can check that, when the births of the two particular years differ by only a few thousands (e.g. 590000 or 595000, as against 600000), the method of the weighted mean produces results much like those from the standard calculation.

1 This estimate is fictitious since 'double classification' does not take place in England and Wales. In countries like France, however, one can extract the number of infants in the 1971 cohort who died before their 1st birthday (i.e. in either 1971 or 1972).

Table 4.2 Calculation of infant mortality rate during calendar year A based on differently weighted totals of infant death

Births during calendar year A−1 (1)	A (2)	Deaths before age 1 during calendar year A (3)	Weighting factors (4)	Weighted mean of births (5)	Infant mortality rate per 1000	
					Standard $(6) = \frac{(3)}{(2)}$	According to weighted mean $(7) = \frac{(3)}{(5)}$
510000	600000	10000	0.2; 0.8	$0.2 \times 510000 + 0.8 \times 600000 = 582000$	16.7	17.2
		20000	0.25; 0.75	$0.25 \times 510000 + 0.75 \times 600000 = 577500$	33.3	34.6
		60000	$\frac{1}{3}; \frac{2}{3}$	$\frac{1}{3} \times 510000 + \frac{2}{3} \times 600000 = 570000$	100.0	105.3

4.5 Comparison of mortality levels: the method of direct standardization

Comparative studies over time and space have a major role in demography. How do we make such comparisons in the case of mortality?

Obviously, two types of index can be used:

the crude death rate for broad comparisons;
the various age-sex-specific rates for more detailed comparisons.

We instinctively feel that the crude death rate depends on the values of the different age-sex-specific rates contributing to it. But can we say that two populations with the same age-specific rates have the same crude rates?

The answer is no, and it follows that the crude rate does not truly reflect the mortality level.

To clarify this answer, let us subject two populations with very different age structures to the same age-specific rates. (So as not to be too cumbersome we divide the population into three age groups only.) Table 4.3 shows the results, and we see that with the same series of age-specific rates[1] the crude rate for one population is almost double that for the other (10.7 per 1000 as against 5.8). This is because of the very different weight in the two populations of persons at high risk of death (20% of the '60 years and over' in country A as against 5% in country B).

The death rate, therefore, provides a comparative index only if the structures of the populations under comparison are identical; this is usually the case only when the mortality of a single country is analysed over a short period, since structures do not change much in the short term. Hence the following French series

1948	12.4 per 1000	1952	12.3 per 1000
1949	13.8	1953	13.0
1950	12.7	1954	12.0
1951	13.4		

---

1 Each of these large age groups (0–19, 20–59, 60 years and over) will in all probability have a quite different composition, e.g. the proportion of those aged 0–4 in the 0–19 group will not be the same in population A as in population B. Thus, our criticisms of the crude rate also hold for the rate at 0–19 (and for 20–59, and 60 years and over): the same rate of 2 per 1000 for

Table 4.3   Age-specific mortality rates and crude death rates in two populations

Age group (*years*)	Mortality rate per 1000 (1)	Population of developed country (A)		Population of developing country (B)	
		Structure (2)	Deaths (1) × (2)	Structure (3)	Deaths (1) × (3)
0–19	2	2 500	5	5 000	10
20–59	4	5 500	22	4 500	18
60 and over	40	2 000	80	500	20
Total		10 000	107	10 000	58

obviously shows variations in the risk of dying during those years; the excess mortality apparent in 1949, 1951 and 1953 is the result of influenza epidemics.

In every other case we must create a comparative index involving the 'reconstruction' of the crude rates of the populations under comparison on the basis of an age structure common to them all. We can use an example which shows the general application of the method rather well: let us compare the mortality of French medical practitioners[1] with that of the entire French population.

The year of reference is 1961. However, since it is just a single year, the calculation of age-specific rates (even for 5-year groups) loses its significance when the total population is as small as 40 000 medical practitioners. We are bound to extend our observation over several consecutive years: in this case the 4-year period around 1961, i.e. from 1 July 1959 to 1 July 1963.[2] Thus,

the entire 0–19 age group does not mean the same rates at age 0, age 1, age 2 . . ., age 19, in population A as in population B. But let us ignore this objection and assume that the internal structures of the three large groups are the same – this emphasizes the artificial nature of our example and does not detract from its value as such.

1 Specifically those medical practitioners who are (or were before retirement) actively engaged in general practice and who therefore contribute (or did so) to a pension scheme able to provide us with good data.

2 Strictly speaking, to make a comparison in every sense, we should have done the same with the total population, e.g. the French crude rate is 10.8 per 1000 in 1961 but rises to 11.2 for the 4-year period. We did not do so for reasons of simplicity; it obviously does not affect our explanation of the method.

Table 4.4 Mortality rates of the entire French population and of French medical practitioners

Age group (years)	France (1961)			Medical practitioners (mid-1959 to mid-1963)		
	Population (000s)	Deaths	Rate per 1000	Medical practitioner- years	Deaths	Rate per 1000
30–34	3285.0	5408	1.6	22833	26	1.1
35–39	3276.2	7257	2.2	29506	59	2.0
40–44	2311.1	6903	3.0	18561	31	1.7
45–49	2607.9	13343	5.1	18984	83	4.4
50–54	2914.8	23070	7.9	18865	106	5.6
55–59	2803.1	34093	12.2	12594	136	10.8
60–64	2430.9	44078	18.1	9629	176	18.3
65–69	1879.0	49382	26.3	7834	214	27.3
70–74	1503.2	63576	42.3	7245	355	49.0
75–79	1085.4	76857	70.8	5245	353	67.3
80–84	624.7	69762	111.6	3524	356	101.0
85–89	254.0	46812	184.2	1644	272	165.5
90 and over	62.4	18375	294.4	448	107	238.8
Total	28037.7	458916	16.4	156912	2274	14.5

for each age group, we can

> either reduce the deaths of the period to an average annual number (divide by 4) and relate them to the mean population, i.e. on 1 July 1961;
>
> or relate the total deaths recorded to the number of medical practitioner-years at risk, i.e. (see p. 37) the number of medical practitioners at risk of dying during whole years within the period (thus, a practitioner under observation for 3 of the 4 years counts as 3 units).

These two procedures are absolutely equivalent, but it is the second which is used on the right-hand side of Table 4.4 (the total number of medical practitioner-years – 156912 – is four times the average number of practitioners for the period – 39228).[1]

The number of medical practitioners aged under 30 is negligible (it does not appear in Table 4.4), so that we calculate the crude rate in both the entire and the practitioner population for those aged 30 and over. The rate is 16.4 in the French population and 14.5 per 1000 among the medical practitioners; would this difference remain if both populations had the same age structure?

1 We do not delve into detail here about how to calculate medical practitioner-years: this would lead to a long digression about a simple problem. We shall return to it, in terms of women-years at risk, in chapter 6 on fertility.

Table 4.5   Mortality rates of the population of medical
practitioners applied to the age structure of the French population
(1961)

Age group (*years*)	French population (000s) (1)	Medical practitioner age-specific mortality rates per 1000 (2)	Expected deaths (1) × (2)
30–34	3285.0	1.1	3614
35–39	3276.2	2.0	6552
40–44	2311.1	1.7	3929
45–49	2607.9	4.4	11475
50–54	2914.8	5.6	16323
55–59	2803.1	10.8	30273
60–64	2430.9	18.3	44485
65–69	1879.0	27.3	51297
70–74	1503.2	49.0	73657
75–79	1085.4	67.3	73047
80–84	624.7	101.0	63095
85–89	254.0	165.5	42037
90 and over	62.4	238.8	14901
Total	28037.7	*15.5*	434685

To answer this question, we must first choose an age structure
common to both populations. There is no compelling reason for
a particular choice. However, we should note that when we choose
one of the two populations in question as the *standard population*,
e.g. the French one, we do not need to recalculate its crude death
rate. The result (see Table 4.5) is now a crude death rate of 15.5
per 1000, which may be called the *standardized mortality rate*:
this is the crude death rate of medical practitioners using the
entire French population as the standard population. Thus, the
initial difference between 16.4 and 14.5 has been reduced to the
difference between 16.4 and 15.5 without, as is sometimes the
case, being reversed. We could also have chosen the population of
medical practitioners as the standard one; if so, it would have
been the crude death rate of the French population that would
have altered: calculation shows that we would have had 15.6
instead of 16.4 to compare with 14.5.

Table 4.6 provides a useful summary of these various comparisons. Reading diagonally we have the result of the direct

Table 4.6   Crude death rates on the basis of different combinations of population structures and age-specific rates per 1000

		Population structure	
		France	Medical practitioners
Age-specific rates	France	16.4	15.6
	Medical practitioners	15.5	14.5

comparison (16.4 and 14.5); the comparisons using the same population structure appear in the same column. Note that the difference is very similar whether we choose the French population structure (0.9 per 1000) or the structure of medical practitioners (1.1 per 1000).[1]

This method of comparison, called *direct standardization* (or the *standard population method*), may be extended to cover any number of populations. In principle, we can apply it every time we wish to eliminate the effects of population structure, and thus its use extends beyond the study of mortality. However, it is in the context of demographic phenomena that the method is most common and least disputed. Its weak point – we do not need to exaggerate the consequences – is the arbitrary way in which the operative age structure is chosen.

4.6   Comparison of mortality levels: the method of indirect standardization

For various reasons, we sometimes do not know the age-specific mortality rates of the populations to be compared (because the age distribution of deaths is not available or because the population is so small that this sort of breakdown would be ridiculous), though we do know the total number of deaths. In such cases we employ the method of *indirect standardization* using a *standard mortality schedule*. To show this method in operation, let us compare mortality in a London parish at the beginning of the

1 Since there are more male than female practitioners, it seemed obvious to compare the former and the French male population; in fact this showed an even lower mortality among practitioners.

Table 4.7   Expected number of deaths on the basis of a standard mortality schedule

Age group (years)	London parish population (1)	French age-specific rates per 1000 (2)	Expected deaths (1) × (2)
Under 1	210	231*	49
1–4	786	40	31
5–14	1791	10	18
15–24	1510	10	15
25–34	1301	9	12
35–44	942	15	14
45–54	553	23	13
55–64	490	39	19
65–74	173	75	13
75 and over	46	150	7
Total	7802		191

* This is the ratio of deaths at age 0–1 to the mean population aged 0 completed year. It is a rate in the strict sense of the term but not the one already referred to as infant mortality rate.

seventeenth century[1] with that of the entire French population at the beginning of the nineteenth century. Apart from the distribution of the population by large age groups, nothing is known about this London parish except that the total number of deaths is 155 (an average over 3 years). The age-specific mortality rates for the French population give a *standard mortality schedule* which, when applied to the London population (see Table 4.7), gives a total of 191 deaths (those which would occur if the age-specific mortality was that in France). Thus we obtain for the London population a *comparative mortality index* of

$$\frac{155}{191} = 0.81,$$

the index for France, of course, being 1. So the mortality level is visibly lower in the first population than in the second.

1 Data from M. F. and T. H. Hollingsworth, 'Plague mortality rates by age and sex in the parish of St Botolph's', *Population Studies*, vol. 25 (1971), pp. 131–46.

The method may of course be extended to any number of populations; the choice of the standard mortality schedule, just as the choice of a standard population, allows a certain amount of latitude.[1]

---

1 Note that with two populations – and only with two – if, as before, we choose the age-specific mortality of one of them as a standard mortality schedule, we must make the same calculations as when we applied the standard population schedule (Table 4.5), although we are using them differently. The reader can, as an exercise, apply the standard population method to Table 4.7, and the standard mortality schedule to Table 4.5.

5 The life table

The life table is a simple and fundamental tool in demographic analysis, and is used in many connections. We cannot deal with all the problems of constructing one but we can easily get to know its main uses.

5.1 The main features of a life table

A general introduction to the life table, using as an example the French female birth cohort of 1820, may be found in the author's

Calendar year	Age reached (years)	Population
1750	0	10000
1751	1	7675
1752	2	6718
1753	3	6247
1754	4	5987
1755	5	5832
....	..	.....
1770	20	5022
....	..	.....
1800	50	2971
....	..	.....
1835	85	119
....	..	...
1850	100	2

Population, referred to earlier. Here we shall consider Duvillard's historic work. At the beginning of the nineteenth century Duvillard employed very indirect methods to calculate a life table based, it is thought, on French persons (of both sexes) who lived during the second half of the eighteenth century. To focus better, let us suppose that the table relates to a cohort born in 1750 and shows reductions, year after year, in the survivors of an initial group of 10 000 new-borns.

To present a life table in the usual way, we retain from the above data the ages x (birthdays) and the population at each age x, i.e. the *survivors* l_x. The *deaths* between successive ages d_x and the *probabilities of dying* q_x are derived from these as follows:

$$d_x = l_x - l_{x+1}$$

$$q_x = \frac{d_x}{l_x}$$

Since the probabilities refer to a single year of age, they are sometimes specified as *annual* probabilities of dying.

With Duvillard's data we can produce the following table (extracts):

Age (years) x	Survivors at age x l_x	Deaths between x and x+1 d_x	Probabilities of dying between x and x+1 per 1000 q_x
0	10000	2325	232.5
1	7675	957	124.7
2	6718	471	70.1
3	6247	260	41.6
4	5987	155	25.9
5	5832	102	17.5
.	.....	...	....
20	5022	59	11.7
..	.....	..	....
50	2971	77	25.9
..	.....	..	....
85	119	27	227.0
..	...	..	....
100	2		

Thus,

$$l_1 = 7675 \quad \text{and} \quad l_2 = 6718.$$

Therefore,

$$d_1 = l_1 - l_2 = 7675 - 6718 = 957$$

and

$$q_1 = \frac{d_1}{l_1} = \frac{957}{7675} = 0.1247.$$

We see almost at once that

$$q_0 = 0.2325 \text{ or } 232.5 \text{ per } 1000$$

and that q_0 is the same as the index we more crudely called an infant mortality rate (the proportion among new-borns of those who die before age 1; see section 4.3); in the standard notation used in life tables it is known as the probability of death at age 0. Although because of special use of language the words 'rate' and 'probability' here mean one and the same thing, by strict definition the two indexes do refer to two different, albeit closely connected, quantities; we shall go into this later.

In our example we derived the d_x and q_x series from l_x, the series of survivors. In fact, we can, from any one of these series, derive the other two. Note particularly that from the q_x series we can reconstruct those of l_x and d_x. Thus, having l_0 we obtain:

$$d_0 = l_0 \times q_0,$$

then

$$l_1 = l_0 - d_0,$$

then

$$d_1 = l_1 \times q_1, \text{ etc.}$$

In a less abstract way, if we take the two probabilities q_0 and q_1 calculated above, with $l_0 = 10000$ as the *radix* (or *root*) of the table (a multiple of 10 is always used),

$$d_0 = 10000 \times 0.2325 = 2325,$$

then

$$l_1 = 10000 - 2325 = 7675,$$

then

$$d_1 = 7675 \times 0.1247 = 957, \text{ etc.}$$

Table 5.1   Abridged version of Duvillard's life table

Age x	l_x	d_x	q_x *per 1000*
0	10000	2325	232.5
1	7675	957	124.7
5	5832	102	17.5
10	5511	42	7.6
15	5290	50	9.5
20	5022	59	11.7
25	4714	65	13.8
30	4382	68	15.5
35	4040	69	17.1
40	3694	70	18.9
45	3341	73	21.8
50	2971	77	25.9
55	2572	84	32.7
60	2136	92	43.1
65	1664	97	58.3
70	1177	96	81.6
75	717	83	116.0
80	347	58	167.0
85	119	27	227.0
90	38	7	—
95	11	2	—
100	2	—	—

A life table giving data for a complete series of exact ages is called a *complete life table*; in other cases we refer to an *abridged life table*. Table 5.1 is an example of the latter derived from data in Duvillard's complete life table; we retain ages which usually appear in an abridged one.

Lastly, we should note that the l_x series on its own constitutes a *survival table*. This has very many uses, and in particular, as we shall see, it is from this table that we can conveniently generalize the idea of probability.

5.2   The mortality rate and the probability of dying

The difference between these two concepts is not always clear, and an example will explain it.

Let us take a birth cohort, e.g. the one undergoing the mortality set out in Duvillard's table. At age 5 there are 5832 survivors and at age 6, 5730. We can determine a *rate* at age 5 completed years, i.e. for mortality between ages 5 and 6, by relating the deaths between these two ages to the mean population, i.e. the arithmetic mean of the survivors at ages 5 and 6.[1] Thus, we obtain:

deaths: $5832 - 5730 = 102$,

mean population: $\dfrac{5832 + 5730}{2} = 5781$,

rate at age 5 completed years: $\dfrac{102}{5781} = 17.6$ per 1000.

Probability q_5 is

$$\dfrac{102}{5832} = 17.5 \text{ per 1000.}$$

Thus, the rate and the probability are similar here (17.6 and 17.5; to two places of decimals, 17.64 and 17.49).

Let us make the same comparison using indexes for a 5-year period, e.g. between ages 5 and 10:

average annual deaths: $\dfrac{5832 - 5511}{5} = 64.2$,

mean population: $\dfrac{5832 + 5511}{2} = 5671.5$,

rate at age 5–9 completed years: $\dfrac{64.2}{5671.5} = 11.3$ per 1000.

1 The mean population of England and Wales has already been defined as that estimated on 30 June, the mid-point of the year, although in France the mean population is taken as the mean of the populations on 1 January of two successive years. This is the mean population that is generally used in the calculation of rates. However, if we are concerned with a birth cohort (or group of cohorts) we can, as above, calculate a rate between birthdays. In either case the question is always the number of person-years exposed to the risk of dying during the period considered. Thus, in our present example:

The 5730 persons who survive to age 6 have run the risk of dying during the entire year separating their 5th from their 6th birthday, i.e. for a total of 5730 person-years.
The $5832 - 5730 = 102$ persons dying between ages 5 and 6 have each run the risk for half a year *on average*, i.e. $102 \times 0.5 = 51$ person-years.
Thus, the total number of person-years is $5730 + 51 = 5781$, which *is* the arithmetic mean of the survivors aged 5 and 6.

The *probability* over 5 years is given by the formula:

$$_5q_x = \frac{_5d_x}{l_x}$$

(the 5 on the left is so positioned to remind us that here we are calculating the probability over 5 years from x). Thus,

$$_5q_5 = \frac{_5d_5}{l_5} = \frac{321}{5832} = 55.0 \text{ per } 1000.$$

In this instance the difference between rate and probability (11.3 as against 55.0) is considerable.

With *annual* rates and probabilities the difference is due to only one factor, i.e. the denominator, which is always lower for the rate than for the probability, so that the first index is always higher than the second. If we denote the rate by m_x we have the following equation:

$$q_x = \frac{2m_x}{2+m_x} \tag{5.1}$$

The difference between *5-year* rates and probabilities is due not only to the different denominators but above all to the fact that the number of deaths used in the rate is 5 times lower than that used in the probability; this is why the latter is about 5 times as large as the former. With the rate $_5m_x$,

$$_5q_x = \frac{10_5m_x}{2+5_5m_x} \tag{5.2}$$

These statements are true of rates and probabilities over any length of time, and denoting length of time by n:

$$_nq_x = \frac{2n_nm_x}{2+n_nm_x}.$$

Figure 5.1 illustrates the above comparisons.[1]

All these considerations become a little more complicated when we leave cohorts and deal with calendar years, but the conclusions remain valid and formulas (5.1) and (5.2) acceptable. At all events we shall have occasion to use these formulas later.

---

1 Again there is a conceptual difference: with the rate we are concerned with a denominator that represents on average the population exposed to the risk of dying *over a given time*, whereas with the probability it is the *initial* population we are considering.

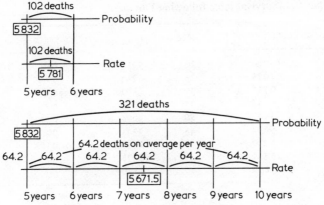

Fig. 5.1   Comparison between mortality rates and probabilities of dying

5.3   Use of the survival table

Table 5.2 gives some relevant extracts from the survival table derived from Duvillard's life table.

The most important thing about the survival table is that it gives the survivors of an initial population (10000 in this instance) at different ages. We can combine these data in various ways to produce indexes of different sorts.

The *probability of dying* may again be calculated from the formula:

$$q_x = \frac{l_x - l_{x+1}}{l_x};$$

thus

$$q_5 = \frac{5832 - 5730}{5832} = 0.176.$$

Using this probability we measure the risk at one birthday of dying before the following birthday.

The complement of the last quantity will obviously be a *probability of surviving*, a probability at one birthday of still being alive on the following birthday. Thus,

$$p_x = 1 - q_x = 1 - \frac{l_x - l_{x+1}}{l_x} = \frac{l_{x+1}}{l_x};$$

Table 5.2   Survival table following Duvillard

Age x	l_x	Age x	l_x	Age x	l_x
0	10000	20	5022	65	1664
1	7675	25	4714	70	1177
2	6718	30	4382	75	717
3	6247	35	4040	80	347
4	5987	40	3694	85	119
5	5832	45	3341	90	38
6	5730	50	2971	95	11
10	5511	55	2572	100	2
15	5290	60	2136	—	—

therefore,

$$p_5 = \frac{5730}{5832} = 0.824.$$

We have already seen that the probability of dying can be calculated for different numbers of years; the same applies to the probability of surviving. Very generally,

$$_nq_x = \frac{l_x - l_{x+n}}{l_x}; \quad _np_x = \frac{l_{x+n}}{l_x}.$$

Thus, according to Duvillard's table, the probability that a person aged 20 will reach 60 is

$$_{40}p_{20} = \frac{l_{60}}{l_{20}} = \frac{2136}{5022} = 0.425.$$

Of course, these probabilities have no forecasting value unless the table used to calculate them has some chance of describing the future state of mortality among the cohorts concerned.

The pattern of diminution recorded in a survival table produces a corresponding average age at death; this is termed *average length of life* or *life expectancy at birth*.[1] If we possess a complete life table, i.e. a survival table without any gaps, and are to

---

1 Once again, the term should not automatically be related to forecasting, as its literal meaning suggests: life expectancies are usually calculated from data related to the past.

calculate the average length of life, we can reason as follows:

Between ages 0 and 1,
l_1 persons have each lived 1 year,
$l_0 - l_1$ persons (the deceased) have lived on average $\frac{1}{2}$ year,
Between ages 1 and 2,
l_2 persons have each lived 1 year,
$l_1 - l_2$ persons (the deceased) have lived on average $\frac{1}{2}$ year. *Etc.*

Adding together the resulting years we find:

$$l_1 + l_2 + l_3 + \ldots$$

$$\tfrac{1}{2}(l_0 - l_1) + \tfrac{1}{2}(l_1 - l_2) + \tfrac{1}{2}(l_2 - l_3) + \ldots$$

which obviously equals

$$\frac{l_0}{2} + l_1 + l_2 + l_3 + \ldots$$

and the average length of life will be obtained by distributing these years equally between the l_0 new-borns, i.e. by dividing the previous sum by l_0; thus, denoting the average length of life by $\mathring{e}_0$,

$$\mathring{e}_0 = \tfrac{1}{2} + \frac{l_1 + l_2 + l_3 + \ldots}{l_0}.$$

Similarly, we can calculate the average number of years of life left for persons of any age x, e.g. 20-year-olds. This we call *life expectancy at x years of age* and denote by $\mathring{e}_x$; so,

$$\mathring{e}_x = \tfrac{1}{2} + \frac{l_{x+1} + l_{x+2} + \ldots}{l_x}.$$

We often have to calculate life expectancies from an abridged series of survivors, such as those in Table 5.1. Then,

$$\mathring{e}_0 = \tfrac{1}{2} + \frac{2.5l_1 + 4.5l_5 + 5(l_{10} + l_{15} + \ldots)}{l_0}$$

$$\mathring{e}_x = 2.5 + \frac{5(l_{x+5} + l_{x+10} + \ldots)}{l_x} \quad (x \text{ being a multiple of 5}).$$

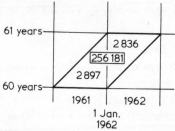

Fig. 5.2 Components in the calculation of a probability of dying (French males)

The loss in precision compared with the results from a complete table is minimal. When applied to the data in Table 5.2, these formulas give (in years):

$$\overset{\circ}{e}_0 = 28.92; \quad \overset{\circ}{e}_{20} = 34.29; \quad \overset{\circ}{e}_{60} = 12.04.$$

Before moving on, we should note that, according to Duvillard's life table, life expectancy at age 20 is greater than that at birth; this is due to the very high mortality risks which new-borns experience in their first year of life. Careful study shows that it is at age 5 that life expectancy reaches its maximum (43.4 years), and at around age 30 that it again reaches the level it had at birth.

5.4 Period life tables

Cohort life tables tend to be historical. Only those tables used in population projections deal with the future of surviving cohorts; they rely, of course, on extrapolation.

Another sort of table attempts to account for the state of mortality at a particular time, even during a given calendar year; it is called a *period life table*.

Period life tables take into consideration all the annual (or 5-year) probabilities of dying that have been calculated for the period in question. Once these have been obtained, they are successively applied to the initial population of a hypothetical cohort (known also as a fictitious, or synthetic, cohort) by the method described in section 5.1. So the only new problem is how to determine the probabilities. There are many solutions but we shall only deal with one.

Strictly speaking, the determination of an annual probability of dying presupposes that we keep a cohort under observation between two consecutive birthdays. Figure 5.2, for example, shows the number of persons aged 60 completed years on 1 January 1962 (i.e. the 1901 birth cohort) and the number of deaths amongst them during 1961 and 1962, which are 2897 and 2836 respectively. Thus, we have:

the number reaching their 60th birthday,

256181 + 2897 = 259078;[1]

deaths between 60th and 61st birthday,

2897 + 2836 = 5733;

the probability q_{60},

$$\frac{5733}{259078} = 22.1 \text{ per 1000.}$$

By proceeding in this way for every age, we obtain a complete series of probabilities of dying and can construct a table, e.g. for the period 1961–2. Figure 5.2 shows that the method we have just discussed does not allow us to construct a table for just one calendar year.

We now leave direct methods of calculating probabilities of dying and turn to an indirect method which meets most requirements. It is based on the conversion of mortality rates into probabilities of dying.

We have already given the formulas – (5.1) and (5.2) – by which rates and probabilities are related in the case of cohorts. Whilst these formulas are very precise for cohorts, they are only approximate when we apply them to rates calculated on the basis of one calendar year or a group of calendar years. That is why correspondence tables (the Reed-Merrell tables) are sometimes used instead; these are based on empirical comparisons which, however, as we shall see, bring about only very minor corrections in the formula results.

For a detailed example of the calculations, let us take the mortality rates of medical practitioners in 1959–63 (see Table 4.4). The first age group whose mortality is known is the 30–34 age

1 Assuming that net migration is nil. But the *entire* calculation will still be correct so long as the migration flows are relatively constant.

group: thus the life table for medical practitioners will begin at their 30th birthday.

To simplify the notation we shall merely use m and q for all the rates and probabilities in question, and so proceed from the 5-year rate m to the 5-year probability q by the formula:

$$q = \frac{10_m}{2 + 5_m} \qquad (5.2)$$

expressing m, of course, in its decimal form (e.g. 0.0011, not 1.1 per 1000).[1] The upper part of Table 5.3 shows the calculations; it is an example of what could be called a *working table*. The probabilities obtained are in the lower part, column $_5q_x$; the rate for the age group 90 and over has been combined with that for age group 90–94, so that the table stops at age 95 (there are 243 survivors at this age from 10000 medical practitioners at 30). By applying the formula:

$$\overset{\circ}{e}_x = 2.5 + \frac{5(l_{x+5} + l_{x10} + \ldots)}{l_x}$$

where $x =$ age 30, we obtain a life expectancy of 45.06 for medical practitioners aged 30.

We can compare the probabilities obtained using formula (5.2) with ones derived from the Reed-Merrell tables (see Table 5.4).[2] The deviations are in fact of little real importance except at advanced ages (over 85), so the effect on life expectancy at age 30 is insignificant (45.07 against 45.06).

Period life tables enable us to follow changes in mortality closely. The average length of life (life expectancy at birth) obtainable from them is still the best summary index that one can apply to mortality levels for a given year. It is important not to confuse it with the average age at death during that year, because this average age depends on how the deaths are distributed among the different ages, and this distribution is partly conditioned by the numerical importance of the various cohorts during

---

1 Note that in order to obtain probabilities between exact ages we must use period rates by age or age group (and not cohort rates).

2 These tables and the way in which they are used feature in R. Pressat, *Demographic Analysis* (London, Edward Arnold, 1972), a translation by Prof. Judah Matras of *L'Analyse démographique* (Paris, Presses Universitaires de France, 1961), with the addition of two chapters from the revised second edition (P.U.F., 1969).

Table 5.3   Probabilities of dying and life table of French medical practitioners (1959–63)

Age group (*years*)	Rate m (1)	10 m (2)	2 + 5 m (3)	Probability q $(4) = \dfrac{(2)}{(3)}$
30–34	0.0011	0.011	2.0055	0.0055
35–39	0.0020	0.020	2.0100	0.0100
40–44	0.0017	0.017	2.0085	0.0085
45–49	0.0044	0.044	2.0220	0.0218
50–54	0.0056	0.056	2.0280	0.0276
55–59	0.0108	0.108	2.0540	0.0526
60–64	0.0183	0.183	2.0915	0.0875
65–69	0.0273	0.273	2.1365	0.1278
70–74	0.0490	0.490	2.2450	0.2183
75–79	0.0673	0.673	2.3365	0.2880
80–84	0.1010	1.010	2.5050	0.4032
85–89	0.1655	1.655	2.8275	0.5853
90 and over	0.2388	2.388	3.1940	0.7477

Age x (*years*)	l_x	$_5q_x$ *per 1000*	$_5d_x$
30	10000	5.5	55
35	9945	10.0	99
40	9846	8.5	84
45	9762	21.8	213
50	9549	27.6	264
55	9285	52.6	488
60	8797	87.5	770
65	8027	127.8	1026
70	7001	218.3	1528
75	5473	288.0	1576
80	3897	403.2	1571
85	2326	585.3	1361
90	965	747.7	722
95	243		

the year (as affected by variations in the annual number of births, migrations and the results of past mortality). The difference between average length of life and average age at death can be considerable; for instance, with a rapidly growing population (e.g. a 3% annual rate of increase, common in developing countries)

Table 5.4   Comparison of probabilities of dying determined by two methods (probabilities per 1000)

Age (years)	Formula (5.2) (1)	Reed-Merrell (2)	(2)−(1)
30	5.5	5.5	0
35	10.0	10.0	0
40	8.5	8.5	0
45	21.8	21.8	0
50	27.6	27.6	0
55	52.6	52.7	+0.1
60	87.5	87.7	+0.2
65	127.8	128.2	+0.4
70	218.3	219.2	+0.9
75	288.0	289.0	+1.0
80	403.2	402.6	−0.6
85	585.3	574.7	−10.6
90	747.7	713.8	−33.9

the author has calculated that a life expectancy at birth of 64.7 years corresponds to an average age at death of 43.65.[1]

The average length of life is not the only index that can be derived from a life table: by calculating probabilities of dying over large age intervals, we can obtain broad but accurate outlines of the structure of mortality by age. We can work out (using, as we know, the survival table) the probabilities of dying between ages 0 and 1 (q_0), between 1 and 20 ($_{19}q_1$), 20 and 40 ($_{20}q_{20}$), 40 and 60 ($_{20}q_{40}$) and 60 and 80 ($_{20}q_{60}$). Thus,

$$_{20}q_{40} = \frac{l_{40} - l_{60}}{l_{40}}$$

This method of analysis is used in the following comparison of male mortality in England and Wales in 1930–2 and 1960–2.

1 R. Pressat, *A Workbook in Demography* (London, Methuen, 1974), pp. 92–6. This is a translation by Prof. E. Grebenik in collaboration with C. A. M. Sym of *Pratique de la démographie* (Paris, Dunod, 1966).

	1930–2	*1960–2*	*Percentage fall*
$\overset{\circ}{e}_0$	58.7 years	68.1 years	
	per 1000		
q_0	71.86	24.49	62.92
$_{19}q_1$	60.00	12.87	78.55
$_{20}q_{20}$	72.33	25.99	64.07
$_{20}q_{40}$	213.94	158.50	25.91
$_{20}q_{60}$	745.38	709.43	4.82

Note that the fall is unequally distributed by age.

6 Fertility

The *crude birth rate* (or simply the birth rate) is the equivalent of the crude death rate; it is the ratio of the number of live births during a given year to the mean population of that year. Thus, with 783 155 live births in England and Wales in 1971, the birth rate is

$$\frac{783155}{48933900} = 16.0 \text{ per } 1000.$$

We have seen that the value of the death rate is greatly affected by the age structure of the population in question. This effect is much less important when we deal with the birth rate, since differences in structure have much less impact on the central age group (ages 20–60) than on those at each extreme (i.e. under 20 or over 60; see for example Table 4.3), and it is in this central age group that we find nearly all the persons at 'risk' of procreation.

All the other indexes which use live births are calculated by relating them to the female population; they are known as fertility indexes.

6.1 Completed fertility

Total fertility is measured amongst women aged 50 (the upper age limit of the childbearing period), in terms of their average number of live births. Although this average number and *completed*

Table 6.1   Completed fertility among different groups of French
women aged 50

	Single persons (0.50)*		
All	Ever	Still	1st marriage at 15–19 *(3.70)*
women	married	married	at 20–24 *(3.10)*
(2.65)	*(2.85)*†	*(3.00)*	at 25–29 *(2.60)*
	Widows and divorcees *(1.50)*‡		

* According to the hypothesis that one-third of births outside
  marriage (illegitimate births) occur to women who do not marry
  before their 50th birthday.
† Women who have concluded one or more marriages before their
  50th birthday, whether or not these marriages still survive at that
  age.
‡ According to the hypothesis that this category represents 10% of
  women ever married, and based on the completed fertility of both
  those 'still married' and 'ever married'.

fertility (also called *lifetime* fertility) are not absolutely identical –
the distinction is, however, very subtle and deviations, for the
most part, quite negligible – we shall here use them interchange-
ably (though we shall later distinguish between *gross* and *net*
completed fertility).

Table 6.1 gives a sample of the very great variety of completed
fertility indexes that can be obtained by questioning women aged 50,
e.g. at a census; since indirect means of estimation are used, they
are approximations rather than precise measures (especially with
the unmarried, widowed and divorced). The results refer to
women born up to 1930 (which assumes, therefore, the use of
extrapolations, since some women would not reach age 50 until
as late as 1980).

Our table does not take into account the births to women who
died before age 50. If, therefore, we had used, not the number of
women reaching age 50, but age 15 (the lower age limit of the
childbearing period), we would have obtained a slightly lower
figure (2.62 instead of 2.65) for the average number of live births
to women over the entire childbearing period, owing to the lower
completed fertility of women who die prematurely.[1] We must

1 This difference is connected with that between *gross* (2.65) and *net* (2.62)
  completed fertility.

return later to this important aspect of the problem of measuring fertility.

Here we shall confine ourselves to analysing the fertility of

all women, i.e. *general fertility*, without regard to marital status, thus combining legitimate and illegitimate births;

women 'still married', i.e. those who remain married until the end of the childbearing period:[1] this is the *fertility of marriage*.[2]

This analysis involves describing the different stages leading to completed fertility, which we arrive at by calculating *fertility rates*. We shall concentrate on general fertility.

6.2   Calculation of age-specific fertility rates

The basic index of general fertility is the *age-specific fertility rate*. This is calculated by relating the number of births occurring to women of a given age to the total number of women of that age. Thus, the age-specific fertility rate at age 20 in England and Wales in 1971 is obtained by bringing together 42015 live births and 334600 women (the female population aged 20 as estimated on 30 June 1971):

$$\frac{42015}{334600} = 0.126, \text{ or } 126 \text{ per } 1000.$$

However, as with mortality, we also come across age-specific fertility rates of a slightly different definition. There is a way of measuring births according to both the age and the birth date (or birth cohort) of the women, just as there is with deaths (see section 4.2). Here are some examples (of necessity, French) of this classification for 1961:

1   In fact, among the group 'still married' in Table 6.1 there are, in addition to women whose first marriage is still intact (a large majority), those who have remarried before age 50. Hereafter, we shall consider only the fertility of those marriages continuous until the woman reaches age 50; we shall accordingly eliminate births from a previous marriage or from before marriage (both of these are included in Table 6.1).

2   We still speak of *legitimate fertility* when dealing with married women (and *illegitimate fertility* with unmarried women). However, the expression *fertility of marriage* is more appropriate when we are considering a particular group of married persons, e.g. those whose marriages occurred during a certain calendar year and whose fertility we measure according to their marriage duration.

Year of birth of women	Age in completed years	Live births	
1942	18	7444	
1942	19	10461	
1941	19	11720⎫	25459
1941	20	29704 ⎰13739⎰	
1940	20	⎱15965	
1940	21	20719	
1939	21	23216	

With the age-specific *period rate* the births to adjoining birth cohorts, with the same age in completed years, are grouped together; whereas with the *cohort rate* we combine the births to the adjoining ages that belong to the one cohort. Thus, for the 1941 birth cohort we have

$$11720 + 13739 = 25459 \text{ live births,}$$

and a mean population of

$$\frac{240300 + 240500}{2} = 240400.$$

So the *fertility rate* of the 1941 *birth cohort* during 1961 is

$$\frac{25459}{240400} = 106 \text{ per 1000.}$$

This is the rate for women who reach age 20 during 1961. But these women can produce live births during the calendar year 1961 between their 19th and 21st birthdays, i.e. at average age 20, whereas the rate at age 20 completed years relates to women of average age 20.5. Because fertility appreciably increases with age in women at this stage of life, this slight age deviation produces an appreciable difference in the rates (106 as against the age-specific (period) fertility rate of 120 per 1000; see Fig. 6.1).

The same is true for 5-year rates. For 1961 the 5-year age-specific (period) fertility rate, e.g. for the group aged 20–24 completed years, works out as follows:

Live births	Mean female population	Rate per 1000
245393	1362150	180[1]

1 The equivalent figures for England and Wales in 1971 are 285703; 1850100 and 154 per 1000.

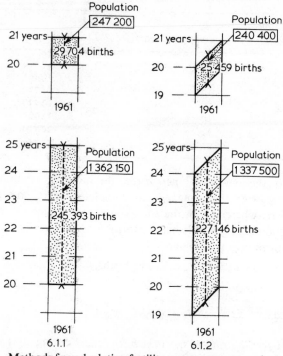

Fig. 6.1   Methods for calculating fertility rates at ages 20 and 20–24 for French females: 6.1.1 period rates; 6.1.2 cohort rates

The corresponding cohort rate is for women *reaching age 20–24* during 1961, i.e. belonging to the 1937–41 group of cohorts:

Live births	*Mean female population*	*Rate per 1000*
227 146	1 337 500	170

Figure 6.1 illustrates these various distinctions.

In France, for fertility as well as mortality I.N.S.E.E. (National Institute of Statistics) gives cohort rates (age reached) and not period rates (age in completed years) in its publications.

6.3   The pattern of age-specific fertility rates

By taking all the age-specific fertility rates for a single year, we can construct a graph. Figure 6.2 gives four examples based on Swedish statistics (see Table 6.2) for the years 1905, 1915, 1925 and 1935.

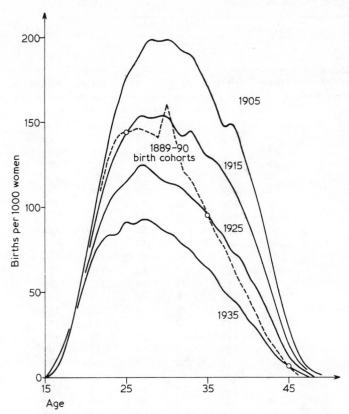

Fig. 6.2 Distribution of age-specific fertility rates in Sweden

The curves have their peaks between ages 25 and 30. They vary considerably in their level: as time passes there is a substantial fall, total fertility reaching 3828 for 1000 women of all ages in 1905, though no more than 1701 in 1935 (see Table 6.2). However, this decline is very uneven according to age: almost imperceptible around age 15, thereafter it consistently increases. These successive deviations in the age-specific fertility distribution are typical of a continuously growing movement of voluntary birth control.

If we examine each successive annual series of age-specific fertility rates, we can easily extract a series of age-specific rates for a particular group of birth cohorts. Thus, in 1905 the rate at age 15 completed years is calculated from the 1889 and 1890

Table 6.2 Age-specific fertility rates in Sweden and France
(per 1000 women at each age)

Age in completed years*	Sweden Year 1905	1915	1925	1935	1889–90 birth cohorts	France 1931 birth cohort†
15	I	I	I	I	I	I
16	3	4	4	5	3	4
17	10	14	12	14	13	13
18	25	27	26	27	29	34
19	45	49	45	42	53	66
20	70	71	63	59	78	101
21	95	89	79	73	98	135
22	119	109	94	80	117	165
23	148	124	105	84	133	184
24	160	136	111	84	143	192
25	178	145	115	92	145	191
26	183	150	120	91	147	186
27	192	155	126	93	146	176
28	199	153	122	91	144	164
29	197	154	118	89	141	147
30	199	154	115	85	160	136
31	196	148	114	83	140	121
32	192	142	111	78	121	110
33	191	146	106	75	116	97
34	181	137	102	69	106	82
35	173	130	95	64	95	71
36	159	128	88	60	84	59
37	148	120	84	50	77	48
38	150	113	74	46	66	39
39	135	103	70	42	55	(32)
40	122	92	60	34	47	(26)
41	106	79	53	29	37	(21)
42	87	64	43	23	25	(17)
43	64	49	32	16	19	(13)
44	45	34	21	10	11	(10)
45	30	20	13	7	7	(7)
46	15	11	7	3	4	(4)
47	6	5	3	1	1	(2)
48	3	2	1	1	0	(1)
49	1	1	0	0	0	
Total fertility	3828	3059	2333	1701		
Completed fertility					2562	2655

* The *French* data refer to ages reached during the calendar year.
† The rates in brackets are extrapolations from a graph.

birth cohorts;[1] these are the cohorts used to obtain:

> the rate at age 16 in 1906
> the rate at age 17 in 1907
> ... ...
> the rate at age 25 in 1915
> ... ...
> the rate at age 35 in 1925
> ... ...
> the rate at age 45 in 1935
> ... ...

This was the procedure we used to compile the series in the '1889–90 birth cohorts' column of Table 6.2. (The four cohort rates which appeared in the four annual series are in *italics*.)

We see in Fig. 6.2 how the distribution shown with broken lines, that of the 1889–90 birth cohorts, 'crosses' the curves relating to the four calendar years: the meeting points precisely correspond to the italicized rates in Table 6.2. Note also the peak at age 30 in the cohorts' distribution; this is explained by a recovery in the number of births in 1920, after the end of the First World War.

By adding together all the fertility rates of a cohort we obtain the *completed fertility* of the cohort, a concept that we have already introduced in a slightly different way.[2]

Thus, the completed fertility of the 1889–90 Swedish birth cohorts is 2562 live births per 1000 women or 2.56 per woman. The same procedure gives us 2655 births per 1000 women in the 1931 French birth cohort, or 2.65 per woman (see Table 6.1).

---

1 On 1 January 1905 the group aged 15 completed years consists of the entire 1889 cohort, and on 31 December 1905 of the entire 1890 cohort; between these dates, the one cohort or the other comes into play in differing proportions. If we had used cohort rates at each age (age reached during calendar year), only one cohort would have featured, e.g. for age 15 in 1905, the 1890 cohort.

2 Completed fertility is, strictly speaking, the average number of live births per woman, in the *absence of mortality*, at the end of the childbearing period (we sometimes go on to specify whether it is *gross* or *net* completed fertility). The effects of mortality can be accurately eliminated by adding together the age-specific fertility rates; the present definition of completed fertility will then be totally fulfilled. It is a little less satisfactory that we previously assimilated completed fertility and the average number of live births per woman *surviving* to age 50; however, as we said at the time, the deviation is minimal and so we shall not differentiate between them.

If the sum of fertility rates stops at a given age under 50, we refer to the *cumulative fertility* up to that age; thus if we add together the Swedish rates up to and including age 35 completed years, we obtain 2.13 live births.[1]

We can also calculate the *average age of mothers at their children's birth*:

$$\frac{1}{2562}(1 \times 15.5 + 3 \times 16.5 + 13 \times 17.5 + \ldots + 1 \times 47.5)$$

for the 1889–90 Swedish birth cohorts, and

$$\frac{1}{2655}(1 \times 15 + 4 \times 16 + 13 \times 17 + \ldots + 1 \times 48)$$

for the 1931 French birth cohort.

In each case the number of births at each age is multiplied by that age, the sum in brackets being divided by the total number of births. The answers are ages 29.8 and 27.7 respectively. Note that according to whether we are dealing with ages in completed years or in exact years, we shall use 15.5, 16.5, etc., and 15, 16, etc., respectively.

Finally, the *gross reproduction rate* (GRR) is the average number of live *female* births per woman in the absence of mortality. It is, therefore, the completed female fertility of a cohort and is obtained by multiplying the cohort's completed fertility by the proportion of female births to all births; this proportion, apparently constant, is usually taken as 0.488.[2] So the gross reproduction rate is:

2.56 × 0.488 = 1.25 for the 1889–90 Swedish birth cohorts;

2.65 × 0.488 = 1.29 for the 1931 French birth cohort.

By specifying how one girl at birth is replaced by girls born to her, on average some 25–30 years later, but *in the absence of mortality*, the gross reproduction rate gives an excellent indication of the ability of generations to replace themselves: in the French

---

1 The group of age-specific fertility rates of a particular cohort and the resulting cumulative fertility constitute what we call a 'general fertility summary table'. The author deals with this in greater detail in his *Population*, op. cit., p. 134.
2 This value derives from the division of live births into 100 females for every 105 males (100/205 = 0.488).

example, the 1931 birth cohort is succeeded by a 'generation'[1] of children whose total number at birth exceeds that of the cohort by less than 29%. An exact measure of replacement is provided by the *net reproduction rate* (NRR), which we shall discuss later. The gross reproduction rate is not in the end a replacement (or reproduction) index but rather an index of fertility, and simply a by-product of the calculation of completed fertility.

6.4   The total fertility rate

It is tempting to treat age-specific fertility rates for a calendar year in the same way as those of a cohort and to interpret the results similarly. This would lead us to refer to the sum of fertility rates for a year (e.g. for Sweden, 3828 in 1905, 3059 in 1915, etc.) as completed fertility, and to infer from it a gross reproduction rate (which we shall later specify as part of 'period analysis').

However, these assimilations, though common, are in general seriously misleading. Strictly speaking, they can only be justified where the fertility level is stationary, in which case what we observe during a particular year is the correct reflection of what we would observe with a cohort (thus, in Fig. 6.2 there are associated curves for the four separate years, which are then interspersed with the curve for the 1889–90 birth cohorts). The assimilations are still plausible when we have reason to believe that we are in a period of stable fertility; and this *cohort analysis* interpretation of *period analysis* data will be correct for as long as there *is* stability. Otherwise the sum of age-specific fertility rates for a particular year must be considered as a simple fertility index in period analysis, and should not be given the significance that the inappropriate name we occasionally meet with suggests; in such instances the *calculation of a parallel gross reproduction rate cannot be justified.*

To deal with all these reservations would lead to the sort of long discussion that may be found elsewhere.[2] Let us just note

1 The quotation marks are because the term is here used in its everyday, and not its strict demographic sense. Note also that we assume a perfect identity between the reproduction of women and that of men, which is never strictly the case.

2 E.g. in the author's *L'Analyse démographique* (2nd ed., Paris, P.U.F., 1969), pp. 119–24. Unfortunately it does not appear in *Demographic Analysis*, this being a translation of the first edition with certain extra matter as specified previously.

that interpreting parts of fertility history based on amalgamating
35 different cohorts as if it were real can lead to absurdities, and
in certain instances might imply a cohort with more first-borns
than women to bear them, or a woman giving birth more than
once within 9 months. . . .

The sum of age-specific fertility rates for a particular year
should, therefore, be referred to as the *total fertility rate*.[1] Below
are the figures for England and Wales, for both this rate and the
birth rate, over recent years.

Year	Birth rate per 1000	Total fertility rate per 1 woman
1961	17.6	2.76
1962	18.0	2.84
1963	18.2	2.85
1964	18.6	2.89
1965	18.1	2.81
1966	17.8	2.77
1967	17.3	2.63
1968	16.9	2.55
1969	16.4	2.45
1970	16.1	2.38
1971	16.0	2.39
1972	14.8	2.18
1973	13.7	2.03

By eliminating the effects of irregularities in the age structure,
the total fertility rate gives a better indication of a population's
reproductive behaviour than does the birth rate. In fact, variations
in the total fertility rate are caused by two factors:

variations in the completed fertility of cohorts;
variations in the distribution of births according to the age of
    women in the cohorts

– factors which generally occur together; it is this that makes the
interpretation of the index a delicate matter. The usual danger is

1 The expression 'average number of live births per woman' should likewise
  be outlawed. In France, following the writings of Louis Henry, they sometimes refer to the *somme des naissances réduites* (literally the sum of reduced
  births – reduced of course on the basis of a uniform number of women,
  usually 1000 or 1 in each cohort).

to ascribe variations in the total fertility rate, only to similar variations in completed fertility. Thus, a fall in the index is commonly interpreted as a fall in completed fertility, whereas it could simply be due to a lengthening – be it temporary or permanent – of the intervals between births.

The interpretation of variations in the total fertility rate is always a delicate procedure despite the guidelines given by certain simple theoretical models.

Finally, we should note that the total fertility rate can be calculated from 5-year rates; for England and Wales in 1971 we have the following 5-year rates:

Age group	Rate per 1000	Age group	Rate per 1000
15–19	51.0	35–39	32.8
20–24	154.4	40–44	8.1
25–29	154.5	45–49	0.5
30–34	77.7	Total	479.0

Each of these rates is construed as valid on average for each of the five 1-year age intervals corresponding to it; on this basis the total fertility rate is given by multiplying by 5 the result of adding together the 5-year rates:

$$0.479 \times 5 = 2.39, \text{ compared with } 2.38,$$

the latter being the sum obtained using annual rates.

6.5 Fertility of marriage

Apart from being restricted to legitimate births, the fertility of marriage differs from general fertility in that we are no longer analysing birth cohorts but *marriage cohorts*, i.e. groups of marriages occurring during a particular calendar year. We can, for a given year, consider all marriages, or just first marriages, or again those taking place before the woman has reached a certain age, e.g. age 50 (here we are eliminating all marriages that we can assume to be sterile). We can also take account of births before the marriage concerned and, particularly with first marriages, the illegitimate births – as we did when we described the completed fertility of woman still married (see Table 6.1).

For the time being, we shall confine ourselves to all marriages occurring during a particular year (first marriages and remarriages), and consider only the births resulting from them. We shall see that the results differ from those for women 'still married' in Table 6.1, since that table gives the total fertility of the woman, and not just the fertility since her last marriage. We must expect completed fertility in the present case to be lower than its equivalent in the table.

Measurement of the fertility of marriage is based on the calculation of *marriage duration-specific rates*,[1] which are a transposed form of age-specific fertility rates. So we substitute

for births among women of a given age, births among women of a certain marriage duration (the numerator), and

for all women of the given age, the number of women of that same marriage duration (the denominator).[2]

However, there is a small difficulty here: we generally do not know the number of surviving marriages that exist during the calendar year for which the rate is being calculated.

Let us suppose we are to calculate the fertility rate at 15 years marriage duration (duration reached) in France in 1961. We are concerned with the marriages of $1961 - 15 = 1946$. But we only know their *initial* number, i.e. those registered during 1946 which are 516900. Now between 1946 and 1961 some of these marriages have ended, either in widowhood (about 6%) or in divorce (about 7%); on the other hand net immigration has brought into France couples married elsewhere, whose children born during 1961 will be included in the year's birth statistics for those of 15 years marriage duration.

Just for example's sake let us assume that the balance sheet of all these factors gives a fall in the number of marriages of about 10% and that the number of surviving marriages in 1961, for the 1946 cohort, should be 465000. We relate the 16937 live births

---

1 It is obviously unnecessary to specify *legitimate* fertility by marriage duration.

2 The distinctions we established between period rates and cohort rates for mortality and fertility reappear here: as well as the rate by marriage duration (in completed years) we can examine the rate by marriage cohort (or according to the marriage duration attained).

occurring in 1961 after 15 years of marriage[1] to these surviving marriages, and obtain a fertility rate of

$$\frac{16937}{465000} = 36 \text{ per 1000 marriages.}$$

However, as we do not know the exact number of surviving marriages (ours is only an approximation) we usually calculate the rate in proportion to the *initial* number of marriages, in this case 516900; we thus obtain:

$$\frac{16937}{516900} = 33 \text{ per 1000 marriages,}$$

which is, of course, an under-estimate (in Table 6.3 the rate of 32 is due to rounding-off).[2]

The use made of rates by marriage duration is exactly the same as for age-specific fertility rates; so Table 6.3 is homologous with Table 6.2.

By extracting, then, from the rates for 1946 the one for marriages during that year, from the 1947 rates that for 1 year of marriage (duration reached), from the 1948 rates that for 2 years of marriage, etc., we obtain the series in the '1946 marriage cohort' column of Table 6.3 (the five cohort rates that derive from the five annual series are in *italics*).

By adding together all the fertility rates of a marriage cohort we arrive at the *completed fertility* of that cohort, or an incomplete sum giving *cumulative fertility* at whatever duration. However, when we use rates calculated in relation to the initial number of marriages, we under-estimate completed fertility; to make clear the difference we could refer to *net* as against *gross completed fertility*, though in practice this is seldom done. Table 6.4 gives an idea of the size of the difference; it also shows the varying results obtained by separating out from the total marriage cohort, sub-cohorts corresponding to 5-year intervals of age at marriage.

Finally, as with age-specific fertility rates, it is usual to add together the fertility rates by marriage duration for a calendar

1 Figure obtained by using a proportional distribution of births where the marriage duration of the mother was not stated (they amounted in fact to 5138).
2 The equivalent rate for England and Wales is 23 per 1000 marriages (16 per 1000 in 1971).

Table 6.3 Marriage duration-specific fertility rates in France (per 1000 marriages in each cohort)

Marriage duration* (years)	Year 1946	1951	1956	1961	1966	1946 marriage cohort
Year of marriage	114	129	134	133	147	114
1	412	410	414	430	426	426
2	273	269	277	288	285	270
3	227	219	233	247	243	227
4	200	189	203	215	213	198
5	174	162	175	184	179	162
6	159	138	151	159	157	139
7	155	125	125	136	131	118
8	153	106	104	114	109	103
9	133	91	86	98	91	86
10	117	80	74	85	78	74
11	99	65	62	73	68	65
12	84	55	61	59	57	54
13	71	52	51	49	49	47
14	61	45	44	40	41	38
15	50	38	38	32	34	32
16	42	32	29	27	30	26
17	33	27	22	27	23	21
18	26	22	19	22	17	17
19	20	17	14	17	13	12
20	14	14	11	13	9	9
Over 20	29	26	23	24	26	25
Total fertility	2646	2311	2350	2472	2426	
Completed fertility						2263

* Duration reached during the calendar year.

Table 6.4 Completed fertility of marriage cohorts constituted up to 1950 in France

	All ages	Women married at 15–19 years	20–24 years	25–29 years	30–34 years	35–39 years	40–49 years
Net completed fertility	2.40	3.47	2.72	2.14	1.55	0.88	0.20
Gross completed fertility	2.52	3.71	2.86	2.23	1.60	0.90	0.20

Table 6.5   Age-specific fertility rate and legitimate fertility rate at
age 20 (age reached) for England and Wales in 1971

	Total female population	Married female population
Live births (1)	38056	32449
Mean population (2)	328900	100200
Fertility rate (1):(2)	116 (per 1000)	324

year to obtain a period index of the fertility of marriage, the
variations in which may also have a double origin: changes in the
completed fertility of cohorts and in the distribution of births by
marriage duration within the cohorts. Here again, we must be
careful not to interpret these annual aggregates as if they had the
significance of completed fertility; such assimilation is valid only
in the case of stationary – or almost stationary – fertility.[1]

6.6   Age-specific legitimate fertility rates

It would seem logical to study legitimate fertility not with measures
derived from marriage cohorts, but by recourse to birth cohorts
and to the calculation of *age-specific legitimate fertility rates* by
relating:

the legitimate births of a calendar year among women of a
given age, to

the total number of married women of that age (mean population).

Table 6.5 illustrates such a calculation and compares it with the
age-specific fertility rate. The legitimate fertility rate is obviously
always higher than the general fertility rate, particularly at
younger ages.

Calculation of the age-specific legitimate fertility rate is justified
if age is the main variable determining a married woman's
fertility. This is true of populations not practising birth control,
but untrue otherwise.

1 It is just as incorrect to speak of the 'average number of live births per
marriage', and we must retain the expression 'total fertility rate by marriage
duration'.

Age obviously controls the ability to procreate because of the interval (from a little under age 15 up to about age 50) outside which a woman is always sterile and because the ability itself varies with age during that interval.

Marriage, of course, allows full scope to reproductive ability but seldom in developed countries do couples take complete advantage of this: sooner or later they endeavour to have no more children, when they have reached their own ideal family size, which is usually very much smaller than they are capable of. So a woman's age is no longer the only variable affecting reproductive behaviour: the number of children already born is a factor, and this in turn depends on the *marriage duration*; in women of the same age, e.g. 30, fertility will differ between a group married for 10 years and a group only recently married.

On the other hand, in societies not practising birth control, where consequently no restrictive behaviour interferes with physiology, a woman's fertility is in strict relation to her age.

Therefore,

In societies practising birth control, we must study legitimate fertility with reference to marriage duration and not to women's ages. It is interesting, all the same, to examine how fertility can vary, *with the same marriage duration,* according to the woman's age or to her age at marriage (which comes to the same thing): e.g. taking women who have been married for 10 years, and comparing the fertility of the sub-groups who married at age 20 and at age 30; in this way we can examine the differences in completed fertility for sub-groups defined by age at marriage (see Table 6.4).

In societies not practising birth control, we must study legitimate fertility according to women's ages (since in most cases of women of the same age, when we try to show differences by marriage duration attributable to physiological factors, there is no result).

Populations not practising birth control, for which we have to calculate age-specific legitimate fertility rates, are generally either earlier European populations or those of today's developing countries. It is rare in both cases to have data from such systematic returns of large populations as are shown in Table 6.5. Instead we have to reconstruct the women's childbearing history either by extracting data from registers (in the case of earlier European populations) or by using a retrospective survey (in the case of populations of the Third World) in order to obtain the rates. Let us briefly examine the specific calculation problems that arise.

We shall confine ourselves to a case where the data collected are extremely accurate. Accordingly, we must observe a woman from the moment of her marriage and for as long as we are certain that she is still married and that her resulting births are known to us.[1] If the union is prematurely ended by the husband's death (i.e. from our point of view, before she is 50), we may or may not extend our observation a further 9 months, either to take account or not of possible births conceived during the last 9 months of the marriage.[2]

We must take account of:

live births; and of

woman-years related to these live births (equivalent to the mean population used in the standard calculation of a rate). For this (the only thing that may be difficult), we should bring together the different dates in question: the woman's birth date, the date of her marriage, of her live births and of her husband's death, e.g.

(A) Woman's own birth	13 June 1896
(B) Marriage	29 May 1918
(C) First live birth	5 November 1919
(D) Second live birth	28 June 1923
(E) Husband's death	17 March 1934.

From this we can give the woman's age in *completed years* as follows: 21 at event B, 23 at C, 27 at D and 37 at E. We can now move on to accurate *average* ages at the various times by considering what took place at age 21 completed years as having done so

---

1 This raises the difficult question of the criteria for choosing the woman from amongst the particular population. See M. Fleury and L. Henry, *Nouveau manuel de dépouillement et d'exploitation de l'état civil ancien* (Paris, I.N.E.D., 1965), and in English, 'Family reconstitution', in E. A. Wrigley (ed.), *Introduction to English Historical Demography* (London, Weidenfeld and Nicolson, 1966), ch. 4.

2 Our choice must obviously be the same for all women, whether they produce posthumous children or not, since to include only those who have such a birth would bring in a systematic bias.

at average age 21.5, what took place at age 23 completed years as having done so at average age 23.5, and so on; thus we sometimes over-estimate and sometimes under-estimate the actual duration, but on average so long as we work on a certain number of observations we can expect them to cancel each other out.

Accordingly, we can take the above woman, place her amongst women married at age 20–24 and assign to her the following woman-years (WY) and live births (B):

Age groups (years)

20–24		25–29		30–34		35–39[1]	
WY	B	WY	B	WY	B	WY	B
3.5	1	5	1	5	0	2.5	0

If we take all the married women in the 20–24 age group in a given population, we obtain results of the following type:[2]

	20–24		25–29		30–34	
	WY	B	WY	B	WY	B
Fertility rate per 1000	480	22	1045	48	835	31
	458		459		371	

	35–39		40–44		45–49	
	WY	B	WY	B	WY	B
Fertility rate per 1000	655	20	555	7	245	1
	305		126		4	

We can treat these 5-year rates in the same way as the 5-year age-specific fertility rates (see p. 81) in order to obtain the completed fertility of women married at age 20:

$$5(458 + 459 + 371 + 305 + 126 + 4) = 10615, \text{ or } 10.6 \text{ live births.}$$

1 The possible number of posthumous live births is not taken into account here.

2 From J. Ganiage, 'Trois villages de l'Ile-de-France', *Cahier de travaux et documents* no. 40 (Paris I.N.E.D., 1963).

6.7   Other measures of fertility

There are many other measures of fertility, whether obtained from more refined calculations than those above, or from very basic general data. Here are some examples.

The *general fertility rate*, the first improvement on the crude birth rate as an indicator of fertility, is the ratio of live births in a given year to the number of women of childbearing age, i.e. the group aged 15–49 (though this is sometimes reduced to 15–44 since fertility at age 45–49 is very low). Thus, in England and Wales in 1971 we have:

$$\frac{782\,338}{9\,324\,800} = 83.9 \text{ per 1000.}$$

With this index we can eliminate certain distortions we observe when using the crude birth rate, which are due to peculiarities in the age structure. In 1971, therefore, it was possible to make the following comparisons for the Standard Regions of England and Wales (rates per 1000; the general rate is based on women aged 15–44).

	Birth rate	General fertility rate
South West	15.08	82.26
South East	15.43	78.54
Wales	15.80	85.12
East Anglia	15.86	83.59
North	15.98	83.67
North West	16.62	88.42
Yorkshire and Humberside	16.67	88.34
East Midlands	16.72	86.75
West Midlands	17.25	88.49

Some rankings are reversed when we move from the birth rate to the general fertility column.

A properly determined *children–women ratio* can be a good indicator for comparing fertility when all other data are lacking. This is true of the ratio:

$$\frac{P_{0-4}}{F_{20-44}}$$

Table 6.6   Live births among the 1900–9 marriage
cohorts of Great Britain occurring before the woman
reached age 45 (including premarital births)

Number of live births	*Marriages producing the number of live births shown in column 1*	
	Exactly the number in column 1	At least the number in column 1
0	13279	129003
1	18154	115724
2	23617	97570
3	20188	73953
4	15670	53763
5	11172	38095
6	8424	26923
7	6169	18499
8	4401	12330
9 and over	7929	7929

i.e. the population aged 0–4 in relation to the number of women
aged 20–44. The numerator is the survivors from the births of the
previous 5 years (these have been greatly affected by infant
mortality, whilst mortality amongst those aged 1–5 is very much
lower); the denominator is most women who have had children
during the period (women aged 15–39 at the outset, 20–44 at the
end).

Finally, we must say something about indexes which bring in
the *order* of live births: *parity progression ratios*. The simplest
starting point is to consider the *marriages of completed fertility*,
i.e. (primary) families where the woman, while still married, has
reached the end of her childbearing period. Here we can refer
to the results of a survey carried out in Britain which we have
already used in compiling Table 3.3.

Table 6.6 provides the necessary data. The second column
gives the distribution of families according to the number of live
births; by adding these figures together we find that there are
129003 families who have obviously had *at least* 0 birth; by
subtracting from them those who have had 0 birth (13279) we
obtain the total of those who have had *at least* 1 birth, i.e.

$129003 - 13279 = 115724$. Thus, this marriage cohort proceeds from a family size of 0 to that of 1 with the frequency:

$$a_0 = \frac{115724}{129003} = 0.897, \text{ or } 897 \text{ per } 1000.$$

Similarly, by subtracting from the 115724 families with at least 1 live birth those who *have had only 1* live birth (18154), we obtain the total of those who have had *at least* 2:

$$115724 - 18154 = 97570.$$

So, family size moves from 1 to 2 with the frequency:

$$a_1 = \frac{97570}{115724} = 0.843.$$

Likewise,

$$a_2 = 0.758; \quad a_3 = 0.727; \quad a_4 = 0.709; \quad a_5 = 0.707; \text{ etc.}$$

It is these quantities that we call *parity progression ratios*. Like completed fertility, they can be calculated for very different groups of women reaching age 50. Table 6.1 provides just one example: behind its eight averages are concealed eight distributions according to the number of live births the women have had, and to each of these distributions there corresponds a parity progression ratio. We must, however, understand that only rarely are two series of parity progression ratios comparable, and therefore, before starting any comparisons, we must make sure that they are identically defined.

The concept of the parity progression ratio leads on to the determining of period measures of fertility that take account of the order of live births. This gives rise to various calculation and interpretation problems that we shall not consider here.

7 Other phenomena

The demographer must be familiar not only with mortality and fertility, which directly cause population change, but with other phenomena, especially those that have an impact on fertility: the marriage of single persons, separations and remarriages. The study of migration is often neglected in demography, but it does bring into play some methods of demographic analysis. And there are certain other social phenomena more or less related to population questions and open to our sort of analysis.

This chapter therefore examines an assortment of circumstances where statistical information can take very different forms, which often prevent us from using the most appropriate analytical methods; thus there is a greater risk that the resulting indexes will ignore certain basic principles and be valueless.

7.1 Nuptiality of single persons

In some marriages in a given year, at least one partner is single. So we can study them separately according to whether it is the man who is single or the woman. These will be *first marriages* for one sex or the other. First marriages are the great majority of marriages (as much as 85% among men and 86% among women in England and Wales in 1971), so with them we are dealing with most of the phenomenon of nuptiality.

We sometimes, however, calculate a global index known as the *crude marriage rate* (or simply the marriage rate). This is the ratio of all marriages in a given year to the mean population of that year. Thus, from the 404 737 marriages in England and Wales in 1971 we obtain a rate of

$$\frac{404737}{48933900} = 8.3 \text{ per } 1000 \text{ persons.}^1$$

As we did with general fertility, we now bring in as a basic index for the study of first marriages, the *age-sex-specific first marriage rate*. Here, however, there are two ways of selecting the denominator. We can use either the *total* number in the cohort or age group in question, or only the number of *single persons*. Thus, the 45 617 first marriages in 1971 of women aged 20 (age reached during 1971)² can be related,

either to all the 328 900 women reaching this age,

$$\frac{45617}{328900} = 0.1387, \text{ or } 1387 \text{ per } 10000;$$

or to the 228 450 *single* women reaching this age,

$$\frac{45617}{228450} = 0.1997, \text{ or } 1997 \text{ per } 10000.$$

These rates do not just differ in magnitude – more important, they have a totally different significance.

Common sense leans toward the second method of calculation: it seems more meaningful to use in the denominator only those persons eligible for the numerator, i.e. single persons. Theoretical investigation does not, however, validate this choice but rather shows that, by relating first marriages to the *total* number in the cohort or age group (our first calculation), we obtain measures which, if aggregated for a particular cohort, give the proportion

1 But we must mention the more sophisticated index obtained by relating the marriages to the marriageable, i.e. to all single persons past the minimum legal age for marriage, all widowers, widows and divorcees. However, this group has a structure so varied from one population to another (particularly as regards age) that we cannot expect it to improve on the crude rate.

2 Just as with mortality and fertility we distinguish between the period rate (by age in completed years) and the cohort rate (age reached). Here we shall use only the cohort rate.

of women who eventually conclude a first marriage – this proportion being a fundamental measure like completed fertility.

Here, therefore, we shall only employ age-specific first marriage rates with the entire group as the denominator. We shall go into the various uses that can be made of the data in Table 7.1 which lead to the distributions shown in Fig. 7.1.

In Fig. 7.1 the rates for particular years are distributed rather similarly though they reach very different levels. At practically every age the rates are higher in 1946 than in the other four years, with a rise in 1961 after the fall in both 1951 and 1956.

By surveying in turn each annual series of marriage rates, we can easily extract for different ages the series of rates for a particular cohort, just as we did with age-specific fertility rates (see pp. 75–7). That is how we arrive at the series for the 1931 birth cohort in Table 7.1 (the five cohort rates originating in the five annual series are in *italics*). In Fig. 7.1, because the curves for the annual distributions are so close together, we cannot illustrate the complete distribution of the 1931 cohort, although we do show the points where it passes through the five annual distributions.

By adding together the age-specific marriage rates of a birth cohort (a female cohort in our example), we obtain the proportion of women in the cohort who, *in the absence of mortality*, conclude a first marriage. For the 1931 French female birth cohort this proportion is 0.9237, or 92.37%, including all first marriages before age 49 completed years; we thus neglect the marriages of older single persons, but these are not very frequent and we can assume that this cumulative index up to age 49 gives a very adequate idea of the frequency of first marriages. We could, of course, obtain more or less the same result by interviewing 10000 women retrospectively, at the end of the year in which they had their 49th birthday, about their possible first marriage and its date. This procedure, as we saw with completed fertility, enables us to get rid of the effects of mortality, and so to deal only with the effects of the nuptiality of single persons.

The *frequency of first marriages* (92.37% in the above) has a complementary frequency (7.63%) which we call the *frequency of single persons*.

We can, of course, determine intermediate frequencies so as to know the percentage of women already married (or still single)

Table 7.1   Age-specific first marriage rates in France (per 10000 women at each age)

Age* (years)	Years					1931 birth cohort†
	1946	1951	1956	1961	1966	
15	10	9	12	14	12	10
16	60	56	57	77	70	63
17	239	206	180	242	232	220
18	604	500	425	547	572	524
19	1057	862	745	932	1021	873
20	1423	1105	998	1203	1296	1105
21	1671	1199	1150	1408	1312	1188
22	1681	1083	1088	1314	1093	1101
23	1531	873	907	1074	826	950
24	1334	679	703	818	608	732
25	1103	517	537	600	456	537
26	864	392	399	428	330	435
27	674	298	302	308	247	313
28	511	232	234	231	182	238
29	409	179	172	174	141	180
30	341	13?	142	138	112	138
31	274	110	113	110	90	107
32	230	95	91	90	73	83
33	190	72	72	71	60	71
34	155	65	59	61	51	56
35	133	53	51	50	45	45
36	112	45	41	43	38	38
37	91	40	38	37	32	29
38	77	34	34	31	28	26
39	65	29	27	27	25	(24)
40	58	27	25	23	22	(22)
41	50	24	21	21	20	(20)
42	42	20	19	20	17	(18)
43	37	18	15	16	14	(16)
44	30	17	14	15	14	(15)
45	26	15	14	13	11	(14)
46	24	14	10	12	12	(13)
47	21	14	10	10	10	(12)
48	18	11	10	9	10	(11)
49	17	11	9	9	10	(10)
Total first marriages	15162	9043	8724	10176	9092	
Final number of first marriages						9237

* Age reached during the calendar year (or age expressed in calendar year difference).
† The rates in brackets are extrapolations from a graph.

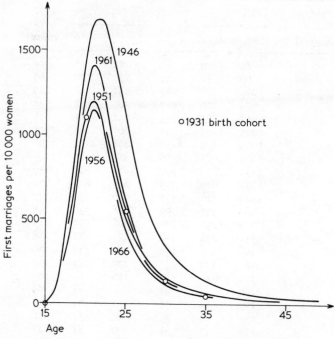

Fig. 7.1   Distribution of first marriage rates in France

Table 7.2   Frequency of first marriages and of single women among the 1931 French female birth cohort (%)

Age (years)	Already married	Still single
20.5*	27.95	72.05
25.5	73.03	26.97
30.5	86.07	13.93
35.5	89.69	10.31

* The figures for those who have reached their 20th birthday take account of all marriages up to age 20 completed years, i.e. up to average age 20.5; the other ages are similarly treated.

at such and such an age. The data in Table 7.1 can thus be used to obtain the percentages in Table 7.2.[1]

Finally, the *average age at first marriage* is calculated as follows:

$$\frac{1}{9237}(10 \times 15 + 63 \times 16 + 220 \times 17 + \ldots + 10 \times 49)$$

where the number of marriages at each age is multiplied by that age, the sum in brackets being divided by the number of first marriages (9237); the result here is age 23.1. Note that if the ages in Table 7.1 had been in completed years, we would have used ages 15.5, 16.5, 17.5, etc, as multipliers.

7.2 The total first marriage rate[2]

By treating the age-specific marriage rates of a calendar year like those of a cohort, we obtain a total we cannot obviously interpret as a *frequency of first marriages*; indeed, in Table 7.1 two out of the five totals would be frequencies greater than unity (1.5162 in 1946 and 1.0176 in 1961) and so would be ridiculous (how can a woman have more than one first marriage?). In fact, here again the interpretation of *period analysis* data using *cohort analysis* terms is justified only if the nuptiality rate is stationary or almost so. Otherwise the total first marriage rate is a simple current nuptiality index and where it exceeds unity this is a sure sign of either earlier marriages (a fall in the average age) or some recovery of prevented marriages;[3] the latter explanation holds good for 1946, the former for 1961.

We have seen that we can analyse the phenomenon of fertility by combining, and creating real biographies from, the relevant segments of some 35 cohorts. This is not, however, possible with first marriages; absurdities arise when the total first marriage

---

1 Age-specific first marriage rates, and the frequency of first marriages which results, are the essential parts of what has been called a *first marriage table* (see, e.g., the author's *Population*, op. cit., p. 132, and also Table 7.3 and the relevant comments below).

2 Sometimes termed, following L. Henry, *somme des premiers mariages réduits* (cf. footnote, p. 80).

3 This point is closely examined in the author's *L'Analyse démographique*, p. 122.

rates exceed unity. Once more, variations in the total are caused by:

variations in the frequency of first marriages;
variations in the distribution of first marriages by the women's ages.

As a final point, note that for this sort of calculation we can again use 5-year rates; thus, for England and Wales in 1971 we have the following 5-year rates (per 1000):

Age group (years)	Rate	Age group (years)	Rate
15–19	83.8	35–39	2.9
20–24	108.2	40–44	1.7
25–29	27.2	45–49	1.2
30–34	6.7	Total	231.7

If we accept each of these rates as valid, on average, for each of the five 1-year intervals of age to which they correspond, we must multiply the total by 5 to get an estimate of the total of the annual rates:

$$231.7 \times 5 = 1159 \text{ per } 1000, \text{ or } 1.159 \text{ per woman.}$$

By doing the same with the French population in 1961 we obtain 0.9955 as against the 1.0176 of Table 7.1 (2% less).

7.3   Percentage single in the population

We have already considered this proportion in chapter 3. Calculated at age 50 (or up to 50) the percentage gives us the frequency of persons remaining single during their lifetime and thus, by subtracting this figure from unity, the frequency of first marriages. Before age 50 it gives us a schedule of first marriages up to the age considered. French data (for females) from the 1876 census provide an example (cf. Table 3.5):

Age	%	Age	%
15–19	93.7	35–39	15.5
20–24	56.8	40–44	13.3
25–29	29.1	45–49	11.8
30–34	19.9		

Here again we must beware of taking the figures as applying to a group of cohorts advancing in age: we are dealing with seven different 5-year groups, each of which has its own history.[1] Also, we must not consider the percentages as characteristic of nupti-ality in 1876, i.e. as forming a period measure of nuptiality. Each percentage stems from the entire past history of the group of cohorts it refers to. The fact that the figures derive from a census and so relate to a calendar year does not in any way reduce the reality and effect of the different histories. On their own they are neither cohort nor period analysis.

On the other hand, if we relate the percentages to a series of censuses involving a particular group of cohorts (e.g. as in Table 3.5), we obtain the real statistical history of first marriages in this group. Table 3.5 was concerned with the 15–19 age group of 1876 which becomes the 20–24 age group in 1881, the 25–29 age group in 1886, etc. If we construe these ages as completed years on 1 January of the census year, we shall be dealing with the group of cohorts which reach age 16–20 in 1876 and whose years of birth therefore extend

from $1876 - 20 = 1856$

to $1876 - 16 = 1860.$

The left-hand section of Table 7.3 gives the percentage single at different ages (we have added age group 50–54, although it does not appear in Table 3.5). These percentages produce the graph in Fig. 7.2, which shows by interpolation the proportions at birthdays 20, 25, etc.[2] The results of these interpolations appear in the table's right-hand section, where

x denotes exact ages;
S_x persons still single at age x from a radix of 1000 single at age 15;
$_5m_x$ first marriages between exact ages x and $x+5$.

1 This obviously does not hold if we have reason to believe that nuptiality does not vary, or varies very little, from one cohort to another.
2 For age 50 the estimate derives from the arithmetic mean of the percentages at ages 45–49 and 50–54. We have also located the percentages for ages 15–19, 20–24, etc., at ages 17.5, 22.5, and so on, though the interpolated line ignores the dot for the 15–19 group since age 17.5 would clearly be too young.

Table 7.3 First marriages in the 1856–60 French female birth cohorts

Age group (years)	Percentage of single persons	Age x (years)	S_x	$_5m_x$
15–19	93.7	15	1000	184
20–24	60.2	20	816	368
25–29	32.7	25	448	188
30–34	21.5	30	260	72
35–39	16.4	35	188	44
40–44	12.7	40	144	24
45–49	11.6	45	120	10
50–54	11.0	50	110	—

Note: in the left-hand section the ages are in completed years and in the right-hand section in exact numbers of years (birthdays).

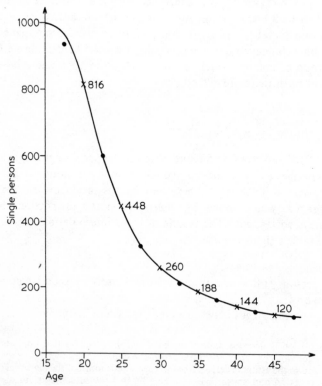

Fig. 7.2 First marriages in the 1856–60 group of French female birth cohorts

Thus, we have put together the main parts of a *first marriage table* for the 1856–60 group of female cohorts.[1] Obviously, the data for the 1931 birth cohort (Table 7.1) are just as amenable; here is an excerpt from such a presentation (age x is expressed in completed years):

x	S_x	m_x
14	10000	10
15	9990	63
16	9927	220
17	9707	524
..	...	...
48	773	10
49	763	—

Lastly, we can see that with the data from Table 7.3 the average age at first marriage is calculated thus:

$$\frac{184 \times 17.5 + 368 \times 22.5 + 188 \times 27.5 + \ldots + 10 \times 47.5}{1000 - 110}$$

$$= 24.9 \text{ years of age.}$$

There is sometimes a preference for age 18 as the average age of marriages between exact ages 15 and 20; if this is followed, the average age at first marriage becomes 25.0.

7.4 Divorce

In French and English law the break-up of a marriage can result either in legal *separation*, i.e. *séparation de corps* (which does not allow remarriage), or in *divorce*. Separation can ultimately be 'converted' into divorce, usually if one of the former partners envisages remarrying. Normally when we study marriage break-ups, we refer to 'divorce' even though we mean all separations and *direct* divorces registered in a given year.

Before we examine the techniques we shall use here, we should note that, if we deal only with marriages dissolved in law, our figures obviously will not give an accurate account of the real extent of marriage instability in a population. Divorce reflects

---

1 The 'main parts' because a first marriage table also contains a series of *probabilities of first marriage*, similar to *probabilities of dying*.

the state of legislation and how it is applied, and both are subject to public opinion; thus, divorce does not have the spontaneous character that marks most other demographic phenomena.

Global measures – our first quantitative approach to the previous phenomena – are of no interest here:

> To obtain the crude divorce rate we relate the number of divorces (i.e. both legal separations and direct divorces) in a single year to the mean population of that year, thus to a group very much wider than that affected by the phenomenon. The resulting index could not possibly be satisfactory.
>
> For other rates (they have no specific names), in which we relate divorces to the mean number of married persons, the denominator is more satisfactory, albeit very heterogeneous, as the persons included are very unevenly affected by the phenomenon. In other words, the weak points in this index are the great variety of possible population structures appearing in the denominator and the usually large number of persons not concerned in divorce.

The significant measures of divorce are those that deal with the marriage cohorts to which the divorces correspond. But there are many obstacles to applying this general principle because of the lack of statistics. The ideal would be for us to be able to construct a table similar to Table 6.3 containing divorce rates by marriage duration, i.e. the ratio of divorces at different marriage durations to the total marriages in the corresponding cohorts.[1] By adding together all the rates for each marriage cohort we would obtain the *frequency of divorces* among these cohorts; by adding together all the rates for a particular calendar year, we arrive at a period index which is equivalent to the frequency of divorces only if, as is seldom the case, the occurrence of divorce changes little from year to year.

We shall here discuss only one method of calculation that enables us to estimate the *total divorce rate by marriage duration*.[2]

1 Just as in Table 6.3, for want of anything better, we use the *initial* number of marriages. In France, what obstructs the calculation of these rates is the fact that there are statistics of divorce by year of marriage for only those divorces which have undergone *transcription* in the population registers. Unfortunately, this transcription is only compulsory if there is remarriage; hence a number of divorced couples do not go through the formality.
2 Also referred to in French as *somme des divorces réduits*.

This is called the weighted mean and has many other uses. We need only know:

the total number of events in question (here, divorces);
approximately how these events are distributed over time (here, the approximate distribution of divorces by marriage duration).

Let us illustrate the method by some simple reasoning.

If, for example, the 33 306 divorces (direct divorces and separations) in France in 1961 arose from a constant number of annual marriages, e.g. 315 000, it would be sufficient, in order to obtain the total divorce rate, to divide the one by the other:

$$\frac{33306}{315000} = 10.6\%.$$

Since, however, marriages vary from year to year, we must relate the 33 306 divorces of 1961 to a mean number of marriages that takes account of annual variations.

To calculate this mean number we shall, in principle, use all the marriage cohorts contributing to divorces in 1961, each cohort having a weight determined by the relative importance of divorces at the marriage duration reached by it during 1961. Here we need a distribution of divorces by marriage duration; Table 7.4 gives such a one arrived at by Louis Henry some years ago.[1]

By adopting this distribution we have

0 per 1000 for the 1961 marriages

14   —   1960   —

28   —   1959   —

...   .

64 per 1000 for the 1954 marriages

...   .

1 per 1000 for the 1926 marriages

Table 7.5 contains all the details involved in calculating the weighted mean of marriages. We thus obtain the following

1 L. Henry, 'Mesure de la fréquence des divorces', *Population* (1952, no. 2).

Table 7.4 Distribution of 1000 divorces by marriage duration

Marriage duration* (years)	Divorces	Marriage duration (years)	Divorces	Marriage duration (years)	Divorces
0†	0	12	48	24	13
1	14	13	45	25	12
2	28	14	41	26	11
3	43	15	38	27	10
4	53	16	34	28	9
5	60	17	31	29	8
6	63	18	28	30	7
7	64	19	25	31	5
8	62	20	23	32	4
9	59	21	20	33	3
10	54	22	17	34	1
11	51	23	15	35	1

* Duration reached during the calendar year (also called the calendar year difference, in this case between the year of the marriage and that of the divorce).
† The year of the marriage.

Table 7.5 Calculation of the weighted mean of marriages in France for 1961

Marriage cohort				Marriage cohort			
Year	Number* (1)	Coefficient (2)	(1) × (2)	Year	Number (1)	Coefficient (2)	(1) × (2)
1961	3148	0	0	1942	2670	25	67
1960	3199	14	45	1941	2260	23	52
1959	3208	28	90	1940	1770	20	35
1958	3121	43	134	1939	2584	17	44
1957	3105	53	165	1938	2739	15	41
1956	2935	60	176	1937	2745	13	36
1955	3127	63	197	1936	2799	12	34
1954	3145	64	201	1935	2849	11	31
1953	3084	62	191	1934	2985	10	30
1952	3139	59	185	1933	3157	9	28
1951	3197	54	173	1932	3150	8	25
1950	3311	51	169	1931	3267	7	22
1949	3411	48	164	1930	3421	5	17
1948	3708	45	167	1929	3343	4	13
1947	4271	41	175	1928	3388	3	10
1946	5169	38	196	1927	3364	1	3
1945	3930	34	134	1926	3454	1	3
1944	2050	31	64				
1943	2190	28	61	Total	1000		3178

* The figures are in hundreds; they all refer to 1961.

estimate of the total divorce rate by marriage duration for 1961:

$$\frac{33306}{317800} = 10.5\%.$$

Here are the percentages for recent years in France:

1946	23.1	1955	10.5	1963	10.1
1947	20.5	1956	10.6	1964	11.1
1948	16.7	1957	10.3	1965	11.6
1949	14.5	1958	10.5	1966	12.1
1950	12.2	1959	10.1	1967	12.2
1951	11.5	1960	10.3	1968	11.6
1952	11.2	1961	10.5	1969	12.0
1953	10.5	1962	10.4	1970	12.9
1954	10.2				

The high values for the years immediately after 1946 are the result of the war: delayed divorce proceedings and an increase in divorces caused by it. Then, after a period of relative stability (1953–63) there is a further increase.

We have seen that if the phenomenon was fairly stationary (as was true of France) during the period concerned, the index would itself be constant and would give the percentage of divorces per marriage. However, in practice the period index diverges somewhat from the cohort index. This can be due to variations either in the distribution of divorces by marriage duration, or in the proportion of couples who end up separated, or to a combination of both. At all events, if the variations are not very important (which is generally true of divorce, except during and immediately after a war), the period index (i.e. the total divorce rate by marriage duration) will give an approximate idea of the frequency of divorces among marriage cohorts, and we shall get a pretty accurate indication if the period index remains fairly constant over quite a long time. Given all this, the above series suggests that the frequency of disunion in France is about 10%. Great care is needed to interpret the recent rise, but we should not forget that it could simply be because we are concerned with divorces occurring at progressively shorter marriage durations.

A similar example might be the 74 437 divorces (decrees made absolute, including both dissolutions and annulments) in England

and Wales in 1971. We can obtain the total divorce rate by relating them to 379 229, a constant annual number of marriages:

$$\frac{74\,437}{379\,229} = 19.6\%,$$

compared with 10.6% for France in 1961.

However, since these marriages vary from year to year, we are again obliged to use Louis Henry's method of weighting in order to determine the contribution of each marriage cohort to the divorces of 1971 (Table 7.6).

We obtain the total divorce rate by marriage duration for England and Wales in 1971 as follows:

$$\frac{74\,437}{361\,055} = 20.6\%$$

Here are the percentages for recent years:

1961	7.1	1966	11.1	1970	16.3
1962	8.2	1967	12.2	1971	20.6
1963	9.0	1968	13.0	1972	33.3
1964	10.0	1969	14.5	1973	28.8
1965	10.6				

Despite the difficulty of interpreting the above rise, we can say that the Divorce Law Reform Act passed in 1971 certainly helped increase the number of subsequent divorces.

The weighted mean method is used very often in demography, and we can also apply it to wider social phenomena. (We shall give an example later.) It assumes that we know the way in which events relating to a cohort are distributed over time; this distribution gives us our weighting coefficients. However, we do not need tremendous precision, particularly if the cohorts in question do not vary much in size.[1]

---

1 By selecting 315 000 in the French example as the constant number of annual marriages, we have a denominator actually located within the range of marriages in France during the 1950s, and the result is comparable to the more refined one obtained using a weighted mean. Such an arbitrary choice of denominator would be much more risky with the divorces of 1950, given the great fluctuations in the number of marriages from 1939 to 1949.

Table 7.6 Distribution of 1000 divorces in England and Wales* in 1971 by marriage duration

Marriage duration†	Divorces	Marriage duration	Divorces
0–2	6	13	38
3	12	14	32
4	70	15	31
5	79	16	30
6	71	17–21	114
7	62	22–26	87
8	55	27–31	52
9	52	32–36	36
10	50	37–41	20
11	44	42+	20
12	39	—	—

* Dissolutions and annulments of marriage made absolute in 1971. In England and Wales every decree of divorce is in the first instance a decree nisi made at the end of a court hearing. It is usually made absolute 6 months later unless a shorter time is determined by the High Court.
† Duration reached during the calendar year.

7.5 Remarriage

Remarriage can follow either divorce or the death of one partner. Statistical analysis of the phenomenon (yet another case of studying each sex separately) here takes on its full meaning when it is applied to groups divorced or bereaved in a single year. Then the following questions must be answered: how frequent is remarriage in these cohorts, and what time intervals separate the remarriages from the disunions which made them possible? It could also be interesting to extend the study to sub-cohorts; e.g. remarriage after bereavement varies according to the age of the new widows and widowers, and so the obvious thing is to examine the frequency of remarriage by age (i.e. age group) at bereavement (new widows and widowers at ages 15–19, 20–24, 25–29, etc.).

Unfortunately, the basic statistical information here is generally very poor, and theoretical principles much less applicable. All the same, let us examine those remarriages in France in 1961 that

Table 7.7   Remarriages of divorcees in 1961 by year of divorce, and the remarriage rate by divorce duration

Year	Direct divorces and separations (1)	Pronounced divorces (2)	Remarriages of divorcees		Remarriage rate per 1000	
			Males (3)	Females (4)	Males (5) = (3):(2)	Females (6) = (4):(2)
1961	33306	30809	4191	2429	136	79
1960	32641	30182	5018	4426	166	147
1959	32261	29924	2185	2166	73	72
1958	33560	31300	1582	1530	51	49
1957	32840	30673	1097	1191	36	39
1956	33743	31254	822	925	26	30
1955	33566	31268	643	717	21	23
1954	32586	30218	542	618	18	20
1953	33379	30996	410	503	13	16
1952	35399	33013	367	465	11	14
1951	35809	33420	352	373	11	11
1950	37023	34663	325	384	9	11
1949	43027	40335	300	387	7	10
1948	48974	45903	293	415	6	9
1947	59324	56292	297	449	5	8
1946	66600	64064	298	458	5	7
1945	40821	37718	121	186	3	5
1944	24773	21544	82	131	4	6
1943	23741	20440	89	129	4	6
1942	20813	17820	43	72	2	4
1941	17656	15898	40	67	3	4
1940 and earlier	(27000)	(24500)	374	568	15	23
Not stated	(33500)	(31000)	636	577	21	19
Total remarriages and total remarriage rate			20107	19166	646	612

Note: pronounced divorces are the sum of direct divorces and divorces resulting from 'converted' separations. We have in columns (1) and (2): along the line '1940 and earlier', approximations for pre-war years; along the line 'not stated', approximations for the 1950s, to which probably belong most of the divorces corresponding to these remarriages.

followed divorce. Here the need to make distinctions among the divorced for a given year is less than when widows and widowers are remarrying; to most of the newly divorced, especially because of their age, eventual remarriage is a real possibility, whereas this is not generally so for new widows and widowers, who are mostly elderly or very old.

The following short account uses French statistics for remarriage by year of divorce (see Table 7.7). We shall, however, be dealing with pronounced divorces, the total of direct divorces and divorces following separation (column 2), whereas we should have liked to bring in all the disunions of a year (column 1), the latter being more representative of the whole situation.

The underlying principle and the procedure are identical to those which produced Table 6.3 (fertility by marriage duration).

Long annual series would again enable us to carry out a cohort analysis (of the newly divorced). However, the results for a limited number of years suggest some approximations for the frequency of remarriage: the two rates in Table 7.7 (646 and 612 per 1000) point to around 65% for divorced men and 60% for divorced women.[1]

Note that when we do not have statistics of remarriage by year of divorce (as in Great Britain), we can again resort to the weighted mean method. The difficulty is to find a plausible distribution of remarriages by divorce duration; but as the annual number of divorces varies very little before 1961, even a very dubious distribution has no appreciable effect on the resulting index. It therefore seems very likely that most remarriages happen quite soon after divorce, and we can select as the total to which the 1961 remarriages belong, the average divorces of the previous 10 years. Thus we obtain:

$$\text{for men} \frac{20\,107}{30\,964} = 649 \text{ per 1000,}$$

$$\text{for women} \frac{19\,166}{30\,964} = 619 \text{ per 1000,}$$

proportions very similar to those arrived at by the more sophisticated method of Table 7.7. The equivalent figures for England and Wales in 1971 are:

$$\text{for men} \frac{42\,438}{53\,148} = 798 \text{ per 1000,}$$

$$\text{for women} \frac{39\,599}{53\,148} = 745 \text{ per 1000.}$$

7.6   Statistical studies of schooling

The weighted mean method can be extended to determining frequencies of non-demographic phenomena. Let us take the problem of calculating the proportion of pupils succeeding in the

---

1 Table 7.7 lumps together those remarriages where the divorce duration is unknown; it might have been advisable to distribute them proportionately among the different durations, but the resulting imprecision is very small. (We shall return to this problem of the distribution of 'not stated' cases on p. 144.)

Table 7.8   Calculation of the proportion of 'graduates' (*bacheliers*) among the French birth cohorts

Age (years)	C	1959 (A)	1959 (B)	1960 (A)	1960 (B)	1961 (A)	1961 (B)	1962 (A)	1962 (B)	1964 (A)	1964 (B)
17	0.10	543.8	54.4	587.7	58.8	594.0	59.4	604.4	60.4	857.2	85.7
18	0.30	490.9	147.2	545.1	163.6	589.2	176.8	596.9	179.0	821.5	246.5
19	0.40	520.2	208.1	491.8	196.5	546.5	218.6	591.1	236.5	625.2	250.1
20	0.15	572.0	85.8	521.2	78.2	492.8	73.9	548.3	82.2	623.1	93.5
21	0.05	572.7	28.6	573.4	28.7	522.3	26.1	494.1	24.7	619.8	31.0
Weighted mean			524.1		525.8		554.8		582.8		706.8
'Graduates'			49 101		59 287		61 381		66 225		86 729
Proportion			9.4%		11.3%		11.1%		11.4%		12.3%

Note: the ages are those reached during the year of the examination.
   C: coefficients;
(A): birth cohort numbers in thousands;
(B): population (A) × coefficient C.

baccalauréat (the French school-leaving certificate) among the French birth cohorts. Here again, if the total of pupils reaching school-leaving age each year were constant, we should only need to divide the number of new 'graduates' (*bacheliers*) by this invariable sum to obtain the proportion we are seeking; but since it is never constant, we must calculate weighted means of the total pupils by using coefficients of age distribution of the new 'graduates' (column C in Table 7.8).[1] We know from another source the numbers belonging to the birth cohorts in question for each year.

These, then, are the components used to calculate the weighted mean, and not the initial totals as given in Table 7.7.

Nowadays the age distribution at the *baccalauréat* should not vary very much, at least in the short term, so that the only variable in the phenomenon is cohort size. In this privileged case the proportions given by the weighted mean can reasonably be applied to the cohort nearest to the average age at the *baccalauréat*, i.e. age 19 in our example, Thus,

9.4% in 1959 can reasonably be applied to the 1940 (1959 − 19) cohort; 11.3% in 1960 to the 1941 (1960 − 19) cohort; and so on.

1 To obtain these coefficients we apply to the age-specific distribution of the top school classes, rates of success in the examination, themselves estimated by modifying the total rate (by about 60–65%) by age: 0.85 at age 17; 0.70 at 18; 0.65 at 19; 0.50 at 20 and 21.

Table 7.9   Pupils in all schools in the United Kingdom (%)

	School year				
Age*	*1962–3*	*1963–4*	*1964–5*	*1965–6*	*1966–7*
14	*97.39*	98.74	99.27	99.69	100.44†
15	43.16	*56.50*	60.16	60.94	63.00
16	23.83	24.48	*25.98*	27.73	29.39
17	12.27	13.27	13.83	*14.75*	16.03
18 and over‡	4.58	4.55	4.94	5.09	*5.63*

* Age at 1 January.
† The Registrar General's estimate of the population aged 14 in England and Wales was slightly less than the number of children who actually attended school.
‡ As a percentage of those aged 18.
Source: Central Statistical Office, *Annual Abstract of Statistics 1974* (London, H.M.S.O., 1974).

We should not leave education without discussing another sort of extension of demographic analysis. Table 7.9 shows the percentages at each age of children in full-time education in the United Kingdom (Northern Ireland as well as England, Wales and Scotland) during five consecutive school years; the percentage at age 14 during the 1962–3 school year relates, of course, to the 1948 birth cohort. Reading the table diagonally we see the percentages of this cohort still in full-time education in successive years (percentages in *italics*). If we accept that the pupils remaining at school during the entire school year of their 14th birthday stay there at least until their 15th birthday, and if we make the same hypothesis for each series of ages, we obtain Table 7.10.

This table has the same structure as Table 7.3 (for nuptiality) and the life table (e.g. Table 5.1); in the present case S_x (the number of pupils remaining out of 1000 at age 14, the last year of compulsory schooling at the time) takes over the role of l_x, and e_x (school-leavers between ages x and $x+1$) that of d_x. We can also calculate an average age for school-leavers by assigning age 14.5 to the 26 pupils leaving before their 15th birthday, age 15.5 to the 409 leaving between ages 15 and 16, and so on.

Table 7.10   School-leavers in the
United Kingdom among the 1948
birth cohort

Age x	S_x	e_x
14	1000	26
15	974	409
16	565	305
17	260	112
18	148	92
19	56	—

7.7 Migration

In practice migration is always defined according to the way in which the area under study is divided: the migrant is a person who, temporarily or permanently, moves from one category of place to another. In particular, we can distinguish between *international migration*, i.e. across an international boundary, and *internal* or interior *migration*, i.e. inside a national territory. In the latter case the area categories used in the most detailed descriptions and analyses are often local-government areas, e.g. the '*communes*' in France; this is particularly true of countries where each change of residence must be notified to the local authority at the places both of departure and arrival.

Moreover, migration will often be measured over an arbitrarily chosen period; we record the location of individuals at two widely different dates, e.g. at a 5-year interval, in order to assess migration between these dates. This only measures *net migration* during the period: some migration will not be recorded when the migrants are counted because some will have returned to the place they started from (in this case net migration is nil), whereas others will appear to have migrated just once even though their final location has only been reached after stays of varying number and length in different places. The relative importance of this concealed migration obviously depends, all else being equal, on the time interval used in the migration schedule. When we establish migration by relating *place of birth* to place of residence at census time, this error clearly becomes greater with increasing age.

Migration analysis can take two main directions:

the geographical distribution of migrants, particularly in relation to the geographical distribution and characteristics of the entire population (distances travelled by migrants, 'pull' and 'push' factors in migration, etc.);

the impact of migration on population movement (i.e. size) in addition to natural movement (caused by the difference between births and deaths).

Let us deal with measures of the latter. The equation,

$$P_2 = P_1 + (B - D) + (I - E),$$

is the fundamental relation between the population at two dates P_1 and P_2 and the events which occur within the interval: B births; D deaths; I immigration; and E emigration. The equation is sometimes given the form:

$$I - E = (P_2 - P_1) - (B - D)$$

in order to assess *net migration* $I - E$. But although B and D are generally known with considerable accuracy, errors arising from the comparison of P_2 and P_1 can be very significant owing to the usual inaccuracy of censuses; these errors, which can be very great because of population size (now near enough 50 million in England and Wales), can severely affect $I - E$ whose size is very much less. We should not, therefore, resort to this type of net migration estimate without great care. Here is what it produces for the period between the 1961 and 1971[1] census of England and Wales:

Population on 26 April 1971 = 48749575
Population on 24 April 1961 = 46104548

$$P_2 - P_1 = \quad 2645027$$

Changes in armed forces,
  in visitor balance, and
  other adjustments $= +130000$

$P_2 - P_1$ (corrected)   2775027

$$B - D = \quad 2709766$$

$$I - E = \quad\quad 65261$$

1 We did a similar breakdown of the population for 1972 (see section 1.1) but there we used mid-year estimates to determine the population on 1 January of both 1972 and 1973.

Similar calculations can be made for a single cohort or group of cohorts.

We usually calculate migration rates in the same way as demographic rates in general. Let us take the population of the Greater London Council area which decreased from 7 761 220 in April 1966 to 7 452 345 in April 1971 because of some 1 085 137 persons out-migrating,[1] some 672 770 in-migrating and a natural increase of 193 492. The average annual figures of out-migration and in-migration are 217 027 and 134 554, respectively; we should relate them to the mean population,

$$\frac{7\,671\,220 + 7\,452\,345}{2} = 7\,561\,783,$$

to obtain

the out-migration rate: $\dfrac{217\,027}{7\,561\,783} = 28.7$ per 1000,

the in-migration rate: $\dfrac{134\,554}{7\,561\,783} = 17.8$ per 1000.

The in-migration rate is not calculated according to the principle behind demographic rates, which require the denominator to be the population leading directly to the phenomenon and maintaining it to some degree. This exception to the rule means that for purposes of analysis we must treat in-migration rates with caution. The advantage of a rate thus calculated is that it enables us to relate the different factors leading to population change; thus, between 1966 and 1971 the population of the Greater London Council area changed because of:

out-migration, at an annual rate of 28.7 per 1000,
in-migration, at an annual rate of 17.8 per 1000,
natural increase, at an annual rate of

$$\frac{38\,698}{7\,561\,783} = 5.1 \text{ per 1000,}$$

the resulting rate of increase being

$$-28.7 + 17.8 + 5.1 = -5.8 \text{ per 1000.}$$

1 With internal migration the terms in-migration and out-migration are used instead of immigration and emigration.

Table 7.11   Rates of mobility per 1000 for the 1891–5
French birth cohorts

Age group	Rate	Age group	Rate
15–19	46	45–49	15
20–24	75	50–54	3
25–29	75	55–59	16
30–34	53	60–64	18
35–39	34	65–69	(16)*
40–44	24		

* Estimate

Source: G. Pourcher, 'Un essai d'analyse par cohorte de la
mobilité géographique et professionelle', *Population*
(1966, no. 2).

The sum $-28.7 + 17.8 = -10.9$ per 1000 is the *net migration
rate*, negative when out-migration exceeds in-migration and
positive otherwise.

To take account of the absolute importance of migrationary
movement for a particular area, we sometimes consider the
volume of migration (or *gross migration*), the aggregate of out-
migrants and in-migrants, and the corresponding *gross migration
rate*. Thus, between 1966 and 1971 in the Greater London Council
area, the volume of migration is:

$$1\,085\,137 + 672\,770 = 1\,757\,907;$$

and the gross migration rate:

$$28.7 + 17.8 = 46.5 \text{ per } 1000.$$

From a rather similar perspective we can examine all the
changes of residence of individuals in a particular cohort, without
reference to their destinations: this is the study of *personal
mobility*, and a *rate of mobility* is defined as the average annual
number of changes of residence among the group in question.
We can easily calculate this rate but are usually prevented from
doing so because of lack of data about people's moves. However,
a retrospective survey of an elderly cohort or group of cohorts
can straightway produce a longitudinal history of mobility,
e.g. the results in Table 7.11 for the 1891–5 group of French
cohorts (the survey was limited to the provinces).

Table 7.13 Inter-regional migration within Great Britain between April 1966 and April 1971 (10% sample)

Region of usual residence in 1966	Region of usual residence in April 1971								Wales	Scotland	Total
	England										
	North	Yorkshire/Humberside	North West	East Midlands	West Midlands	East Anglia	South East	South West			
England											
North	94735	3246	2188	1446	1325	648	4753	1066	385	1482	111274
	85.1	2.9	2.0	1.3	1.2	0.6	4.3	1.0	0.3	1.3	100.0
Yorkshire/Humberside	3630	136300	4022	4046	1876	1081	6257	1736	703	1127	160778
	2.2	84.8	2.5	2.5	1.2	0.7	3.9	1.1	0.4	0.7	100.0
North West	1874	3485	186513	1906	2958	854	8427	2710	3362	1471	213560
	0.9	1.6	87.3	0.9	1.4	0.4	3.9	1.3	1.6	0.7	100.0
East Midlands	957	3501	1628	82174	2585	1618	5737	1932	604	845	101581
	0.9	3.5	1.6	80.9	2.5	1.6	5.7	1.9	0.6	0.8	100.0

West Midlands	1023	1523	3211	3566	140053	854	7635	4072	2112	978	165027
	0.6	0.9	1.9	2.2	84.9	0.5	4.6	2.5	1.3	0.6	100.0
East Anglia	339	782	522	1282	551	37436	5337	1002	312	403	47966
	0.7	1.6	1.1	2.7	1.2	78.0	11.1	2.1	0.7	0.8	100.0
South East	3372	4760	6489	7343	6275	10992	502965	19399	3654	4614	569863
	0.6	0.8	1.1	1.3	1.1	1.9	88.3	3.4	0.7	0.8	100.0
South West	801	1025	1493	1224	2284	917	13395	93115	1429	1080	116763
	0.7	0.9	1.3	1.0	2.0	0.8	11.5	79.7	1.2	0.9	100.0
Wales	361	559	1779	674	1845	347	4279	2040	64253	434	76571
	0.5	0.7	2.3	0.9	2.4	0.4	5.6	2.7	83.9	0.6	100.0
Scotland	1611	1360	2164	1415	1382	587	6415	1326	399	164375	181034
	0.9	0.8	1.2	0.8	0.8	0.3	3.5	0.7	0.2	90.8	100.0
Total	108703	156541	210009	105076	161134	55334	565200	128398	77213	176809	1744417

Table 7.12   Average number of moves before certain ages per 1000 persons in the 1891–5 French birth cohorts

Age	Moves	Age	Moves
15	0	45	1535
20	230	50	1610
25	605	55	1625
30	980	60	1705
35	1245	65	1795
40	1415	70	1875

By adding together these rates, e.g. as we did with the age-specific fertility rates in Table 6.2, we obtain the number of moves before a given age (as with fertility reached at a particular age and with completed fertility).[1] These cumulations are shown in Table 7.12, which takes account of the fact that each rate applies to a 5-year age group and so must be multiplied by 5 to express all the mobility during the corresponding 5 years.

Finally, let us look at a fairly common type of table (e.g. Table 7.13, on pp. 116–17) which divides an area into a number of administrative units (10 regions in this case) and shows how the individuals resident in the area on one date (e.g. 1971) and also resident there on a prior date (e.g. 1966), are distributed between the 10 regions on those two dates.

We analyse such a table by reducing the *rows* (and not the columns, at least in our method of presentation) to 1000; each relative value thus obtained gives the probability of a person resident in a region at the start of the period and still resident in the country at the end of it, remaining in the same region or moving to one of the others. Thus, those resident in the North region in 1966, who do not leave Great Britain (i.e. the group of 10 regions) before 1971, have a probability of 85.1% of still being in the North region in 1971, and a probability of 2.9% of out-migrating to Yorkshire and Humberside. (This obviously only applies to persons still alive in 1971.)

[1] Note that this survey does not consider moves before age 15.

8 Population change and reproduction

The interplay of births and deaths subjects every population to a continuous process of renewal which is measured in various ways. The most general relate to population growth between two dates. Thus, between 1 January 1971 and 1 January 1972 the total population of England and Wales changed as follows:

Population on 1 January 1971   48 844 400

| Births | 783 155 | } | 215 893 natural increase |
| Deaths | 567 262 | | |

Net emigration $-38\,093$

Increase   177 800

Population on 1 January 1972   49 022 200

These figures have some corresponding rates, i.e. ratios of the different components of population change to the mean population of 1971:

$$\textit{Crude rate of natural increase} = \frac{\text{Natural increase}}{\text{Mean population}}$$

$$= \frac{215\,893}{48\,933\,900} = 4.4 \text{ per } 1000;$$

$$\textit{Crude rate of increase} \qquad = \frac{\text{Increase}}{\text{Mean population}}$$

$$= \frac{177\,800}{48\,933\,900} = 3.6 \text{ per } 1000.$$

The crude rate of natural increase (or the natural growth rate) is obviously the difference between the birth and death rates.

Note that 'increase' does not here imply growth: the word is used in a specific sense, and the increase is negative when there is a fall in population.

Like all demographic rates, the rates of increase have an annual dimension. Thus, to the increase from 47 799 450 inhabitants of England and Wales on 1 January 1966 to 48 844 400 on 1 January 1971, there corresponds an average annual increase of

$$\frac{48\,844\,400 - 47\,799\,450}{5} = \frac{1\,044\,950}{5} = 208\,990,$$

which, related to the mean population of the period thus,

$$\frac{47\,799\,450 + 48\,844\,400}{2} = 48\,321\,925,$$

gives the *mean annual rate of increase*:

$$\frac{208\,990}{48\,321\,925} = 4.3 \text{ per 1000.}$$

8.1   Population change at a constant rate of increase

P_0 and P_1 being the populations on 1 January of two successive years, the rate of increase r is:

$$r = \frac{P_1 - P_0}{\dfrac{P_0 + P_1}{2}} \tag{8.1}$$

How do we find P_1 when P_0 and r are given?

Following equation (8.1) we can write:

$$P_1 - P_0 = r\frac{P_0 + P_1}{2}$$

or

$$2P_1 - 2P_0 = rP_0 + rP_1$$

and

$$2P_1 - rP_1 = 2P_0 + rP_0$$
$$P_1(2 - r) = P_0(2 + r).$$

Thus

$$P_1 = P_0\frac{2 + r}{2 - r}. \tag{8.2}$$

If r had been defined as the rate by which the population P_0 increases during the given year, we would have had:

$$P_1 = P_0 + rP_0$$
$$= P_0(1+r). \tag{8.3}$$

We shall see that this formula is useful in determining the size of a population changing at a constant rate. Now, in fact, formula (8.2) is almost equivalent to formula (8.3); let us check this numerically, e.g. for a population whose rate of increase r, as defined by equation (8.1), is 2%:

$$r = 0.02; \quad \frac{2+r}{2-r} = \frac{2.02}{1.98} = 1.0202$$

$$(1+r) = 1.02.$$

Thus, the difference between the two formulae is negligible. We shall therefore consider that *a population whose rate of increase is r finds its size on 1 January multiplied by 1+r on the following 1 January.*

Let us see, then, how a population changes whose rate of increase r is constant. P_0 is the initial population; 1 year later it becomes P_1 with,

$$P_1 = P_0(1+r).$$

Likewise, another year later P_1 becomes P_2 with

$$P_2 = P_1(1+r),$$

but by replacing P_1 by its value above, P_2 becomes:

$$P_2 = P_0(1+r)(1+r)$$
$$= P_0(1+r)^2.$$

Similarly, we can see that

$$P_3 = P_0(1+r)^3$$
$$P_4 = P_0(1+r)^4$$
$$\cdots \qquad \cdots \qquad \cdots$$
$$P_n = P_0(1+r)^n.$$

This is the formula for compound interest.

Let us use it to determine by what factor the present world population would be multiplied in a century if its rate of increase in recent years (1.9%) were maintained. The multiplying factor is:

$$(1.019)^{100}.$$

In order to estimate it we use logarithms:

$$\log (1.019)^{100} = 100 \log 1.019,$$
$$\log 1.019 \quad = 0.00817,$$
$$\log (1.019)^{100} = 0.817.$$

The number whose logarithm is 0.817 is between 6.561 (logarithm 0.81697) and 6.562 (logarithm 0.81704); thus in round figures the world population would be multiplied by 6.56. From 3600 millions in 1970 it would become 23600 millions in 2070.

Let us also see the length of time it would take for the world population to double; this time x must be such that

$$(1.019)^{x} = 2;$$

thus,

$$x \log 1.019 = \log 2 = 0.30103$$

and

$$x = \frac{0.30103}{0.00817} = 36.8 \text{ years.}$$

Population growth at a constant rate of increase is termed *exponential*, though Malthus called it 'geometrical'.

8.2   Net reproduction rate

We have seen that the level of the crude death rate depends partly on a population's age structure, so that although two populations might have similar crude death rates their corresponding life tables (and life expectancies) could be very different. For the same reason, populations with similar crude birth rates could have different age-specific fertility rates (and completed fertility).

Thus, whilst the rates of natural increase of two populations, or of one population at two separate times, might be the same (with the same birth and death rates), the intrinsic conditions

Table 8.1   Effective births of the 1931 French female birth cohort

Age (years)	Survivors (1)	Fertility rates (2)	Effective births (1) × (2)	Age (years)	Survivors (1)	Fertility rates (2)	Effective births (1) × (2)
15	892	1	0.9	33	876	97	85.0
16	891	4	3.6	34	875	82	71.8
17	890	13	11.6	35	874	71	62.1
18	889	34	30.2	36	873	59	51.5
19	888	66	58.6	37	872	48	41.9
20	887	101	89.6	38	871	39	34.0
21	886	135	119.6	39	(869)	(32)	27.8
22	885	165	146.0	40	(868)	(26)	22.6
23	884	184	162.7	41	(866)	(21)	18.2
24	884	192	169.7	42	(865)	(17)	14.7
25	883	191	168.7	43	(863)	(13)	11.2
26	882	186	164.1	44	(861)	(10)	8.6
27	881	176	155.1	45	(859)	(7)	6.0
28	880	164	144.5	46	(856)	(4)	3.4
29	880	147	129.4	47	(854)	(2)	1.7
30	879	136	119.5	48	(851)	(1)	0.9
31	878	121	106.2				
32	877	110	96.5	Total		2655	2337.9

Note: the ages are those reached during the calendar year; the rates are per 1000; the figures in brackets are extrapolations.

of mortality and fertility – which control the reproduction of the species – could again be very different. This leads us to search for measures of population change which will take these conditions into account, and to expect differences in the results according to whether we refer to such measures or simply to the rate of natural increase.

The fundamental indexes of mortality and fertility can be combined, using the 1931 French birth cohort as an example, by applying to the *survivors* at different ages from 1000 women at birth, the relevant fertility rates in Table 6.2. These calculations (see Table 8.1) give us their *effective births*. The sum of these births is the *net completed fertility* of the cohort; this is less than the completed fertility given by the age-specific rates since the latter is not affected by mortality, which progressively reduces the number of women capable of live births.

The total of 2338 effective births gives us the new-borns who replace the 1000 women and the men associated with them. However, the number of men to be allowed for is hard to determine; it would also have to be estimated for date of birth and is distributed among many cohorts; moreover, we would have to include a quota of men who were not connected with the births.

This is why we determine the replacement of the 1931 birth cohort by reference only to the women and to the number of girls born to them; taking 1000 women at birth, we determine the births of their daughters by applying the *proportion of females at birth* to the index of completed fertility. This proportion is always around 0.488;[1] thus the mothers' original birth cohort of 1000 is replaced by

$$2338 \times 0.488 = 1141$$

daughters at birth.

Measured as a ratio to a single member of the cohort, this index gives the *net reproduction rate* (NRR); so that here

$$NRR = 1.14.$$

The net reproduction rate determines very accurately the likelihood of replacement for cohorts at birth. Replacement is more than certain if NRR is greater than 1; it is not so if NRR is less than 1. It is tempting to say that if NRR exceeds 1 the population is growing, if NRR is less than 1 it is decreasing, and if NRR = 1 the population is stationary. In fact, these assumptions are justified by the concept termed the *intrinsic rate of natural increase* (or the *true rate of natural increase*) which we shall discuss later.

We have previously defined the *gross reproduction rate* (GRR) as a woman's completed fertility taking account only of female births. We can see that GRR and NRR would be equal if there were no mortality, but generally we state that

$$NRR = GRR \times l_n/l_0$$

where l_n/l_0 is the proportion of new-born girls who reach n, the average age of mothers at confinement (for live births only, as calculated on p. 78: 27.7). Here let n = age 28 (in fact n varies very little); then

$$\frac{l_n}{l_0} = 0.881,$$

and by applying the previous formula,

$$NRR = 1.29 \times 0.881 = 1.14,$$

the same value as we obtained from the detailed calculation in Table 8.1.

[1] For every 100 girls, there are usually around 105 boys born, so that the female proportion is: $100/205 = 0.488$.

8.3   Intrinsic rate of natural increase

How, then, can this net reproduction rate be at variance with
a completely different type of measure, the rate of natural increase?
The persistence of certain mortality and fertility levels in a population – e.g. those for the 1931 birth cohort – implies that in the
long run a constant rate of natural increase will appear, brought
about entirely by these levels and derived from the formula:

$$r = \sqrt[n]{NRR} - 1. \tag{8.4}$$

Thus, if the levels prevailing in the 1931 cohort had persisted
amongst future French cohorts, they would have attained a rate
of natural increase of

$$\sqrt[28]{1.14} - 1 = 0.0046, \text{ or } 4.6 \text{ per } 1000.$$

Here we term r the *intrinsic rate of natural increase*.

We shall handle the data for mortality (the life table) and for
fertility (the age-specific fertility rate) for a *calendar year* as we
did the data for the cohort in Table 8.1, so as to ascertain the
period net reproduction rate, i.e. of the calendar year in question.
We need only insert this net rate into formula (8.4) to obtain the
intrinsic rate of natural increase for the particular year; we shall
then compare the latter with the crude rate of natural increase.
Let us calculate for 1971, using once more the 5-year age-specific
fertility rates for England and Wales given on p. 81 and appearing now in Table 8.2. We shall thus be following the usual
procedure of obtaining the net reproduction rate by the use of
5-year rates.

In each age group there is a total number of persons who
survive to the median age of the group;[1] we derive this number
from the 1970–72 life table and multiply it by the relevant age-
specific fertility rate. The sum of such products must be multiplied
by 5 to obtain a result for a single year; and then multiplied by
0.488 to retain only the female births:

$$NRR = \frac{1}{1000} \times 466.7 \times 5 \times 0.488 = 1.14.$$

1 As the ages are in completed years, it is easy to see that the median ages are,
in fact, 17.5, 22.5, 27.5, etc., whereas they would have been 17, 22, 27, and
so on, had they been ages reached during the calendar year.

Table 8.2   Components employed in calculating the net reproduction rate for England and Wales in 1971

Age group (completed years)	Age-specific fertility rate per 1000 in 1971 (1)	Survivors (000s)		(3) = (1)×(2)
		Age	Population (2)	
15–19	51	17.5	979	49.9
20–24	154	22.5	977	150.5
25–29	154	27.5	974	150.0
30–34	78	32.5	972	75.8
35–39	33	37.5	967	31.9
40–44	8	42.5	960	7.7
45–49	1	47.5	947	0.9
Total	479			466.7

We could again use the formula:

$$NRR = GRR \times l_n/l_0$$

GRR being

$$\frac{1}{1000} \times 479 \times 5 \times 0.488 = 1.17,$$

which is the product of the total fertility rate for a year (479×5 per 1000 women) and the proportion of females amongst births; we generally refer to GRR as the *period gross reproduction rate* (see p. 78), in this case that of England and Wales in 1971. It does not add anything to our knowledge of fertility for that year and we see no reason for isolating it as a concept; in any event, its name causes misunderstandings.

The average age of mothers n here being 26, and l_n/l_0 being 0.975,

$$NRR = 1.17 \times 0.975 = 1.14$$

– the same result as in the first calculation. Now, applying equation (8.4), we find:

$$r = \sqrt[26]{1.14} - 1 = 0.0051 = 5.1 \text{ per } 1000.$$

This *intrinsic* rate of natural increase may be compared with a crude rate of natural increase of 4.4 per 1000 in England and Wales in 1971. Thus, the intrinsic mortality and fertility levels imply a greater rate of natural increase (the intrinsic rate) than that actually observed. In other words, we can take it that, because of peculiarities in the age structure of the above population in 1971, the effects on population change of the mortality and fertility levels of that year are not correctly expressed by the crude rate of natural increase. The same may be said of the French population in 1961 where the intrinsic rate of natural increase is 9.7 per 1000, compared with a crude rate of natural increase of 7.3 per 1000.

We must, however, make some important reservations about this view. Reference to the intrinsic rate assumes that both the mortality and fertility levels for the given year can continue indefinitely, so that the very age structure of the populations can finally, through more or less rapid change, harmonize with the mortality and fertility levels, and thus reflect through the rate of natural increase that in time the levels involve, their precise impact on population change. Now, this hypothesis of the indefinite maintenance of mortality and fertility is frequently deceptive, especially as regards fertility. Often the results of fertility in a given year are fickle and it is *absolutely impossible* for them to persist indefinitely. This is true of France in 1961 when the relatively higher fertility (the total fertility rate was 2.81, compared with 2.76 for England and Wales; see p. 80) was due to a steadily increasing number of early marriages and subsequent births; this trend has to come to an end and then, other things being equal, fertility will fall.

The period net reproduction rate and the associated intrinsic rate of natural increase should, therefore, be treated with great caution. The net rate is obviously the same as the cohort rate when there is a stationary situation. It makes sense when the hypothesis of the indefinite maintenance of fertility remains intact; and if, as is probable, mortality falls in the future, the period rate will give an estimate by default of the levels to which population reproduction would rise if fertility continued at its present level.

So it is not unreasonable to calculate the net reproduction rate and the associated intrinsic rate of natural increase when the annual fertility indexes are fairly constant; but we must avoid them as misleading on the many occasions when fertility is unstable.

8.4   Stable populations and stationary populations

The theoretical justifications for the concept of the intrinsic rate of natural increase and its method of calculation lead us on to the *stable population model*. In a stable population the life table and age-specific fertility rates are constant, and any population that experiences constant fertility and mortality from a given time is on the way to becoming one.

We can also consider as stable a population whose annual number of births changes at a constant rate and whose life table does not change; the rate of change of its births is also its rate of natural increase.

Moving on from these generalities, let us briefly examine the stable population resulting from the mortality and fertility levels of the 1931 French birth cohort (Table 8.1). By the calculations on p. 125 the rate of natural increase of that population is about 4.6 per 1000 and the annual births increase at the same speed. If, therefore, at the mid-point of year 0 the population size is P_0, then at the mid-point of the following year it will be $1.0046P_0$; similarly, births will change from B_0 to $1.0046B_0$ and the birth rate

$$\frac{B_0}{P_0} \quad \text{will become} \quad \frac{1.0046B_0}{1.0046P_0} = \frac{B_0}{P_0}$$

i.e. it remains *constant. This is also true of the death rate* since the difference between the two rates, i.e. the rate of natural increase, is equally constant.

Furthermore, the *age structure of this population is constant*. We can establish this by an easy (but tedious) calculation. If we take 10000 births for year 0, then those for year 1 are:

$$10\,000\,(1.0046) = 10046,$$

those for year 2:

$$10000\,(1.0046)^2, \quad \text{etc.}$$

On 1 January of year 3, the group aged 0 completed years consists of the survivors of the new-borns of year 2; they amount, therefore, to

$$10000\,(1.0046)^2\frac{l_0+l_1}{2l_1}.$$

Similarly, the group aged 1 completed year amounts to

$$10000\,(1.0046)\frac{l_1+l_2}{2l_0}, \quad \text{etc.,}$$

the quantities l_0, l_1, l_2, and so on, being the survivors in the (constant) life table.

This is only an outline of the calculation principle; a full treatment can be found elsewhere (e.g. in the author's *Demographic Analysis*, p. 318).

A special case of stable population is when the annual rate of increase is nil; this is known as a *stationary population*. Each year a certain number of persons are born; let us denote them by l_0 so as to analyse the age structure and some other characteristics of this population.

At 0 completed calendar year the survivors are between 0 and 1 exact year old and their total number is somewhere between l_0 and l_1 which we shall take as:

$$\frac{l_0+l_1}{2}.$$

Similarly at 1 and 2 completed year we have, respectively:

$$\frac{l_1+l_2}{2} \quad \text{and} \quad \frac{l_2+l_3}{2}, \quad \text{etc.}$$

The total population, therefore, is:

$$\frac{l_0+l_1+l_1+l_2+l_2+l_3+\cdots}{2} = \frac{l_0}{2}+l_1+l_2+l_3+\cdots$$

and we can easily check that it is constant since the rate of change of the births is equal to the rate of natural increase, i.e. nil. The birth rate, then, is:

$$b = \frac{l_0}{\frac{l_0}{2}+l_1+l_2+l_3+\cdots};$$

thus,

$$b = \frac{1}{\frac{1}{2}+\frac{l_1+l_2+l_3+\cdots}{l_0}}.$$

We recognize that the denominator is the life expectancy at birth, and thus, in a stationary population, the birth rate is equal to the death rate (since the rate of natural increase is nil), both being equal to the reciprocal of the life expectancy at birth:

$$\overset{\circ}{e}_0 = \frac{1}{b} = \frac{1}{d}.$$

B and P denote the invariable numbers for births and population respectively:

$$b = \frac{B}{P} = \frac{1}{\overset{\circ}{e}_0} \quad \left(\text{since } \frac{1}{b} = e_0^0\right).$$

We derive from this:

$$P = B\overset{\circ}{e}_0 \tag{8.5}$$

i.e. the population size is equal to the number of annual births multiplied by the average length of life. Thus, if the 783 000 live births in England and Wales were maintained along with the present average length of life of about 71 years, the population would reach a stationary figure of

$$783\,000 \times 71 = 55\,593\,000.$$

In the same circumstances the death rate (like the birth rate) would stabilize at

$$\frac{1}{71} = 14.1 \text{ per } 1000,$$

just a little higher than the rate in 1973 (13.7 per 1000), while the life table by hypothesis remains constant. This difference is explained by a very slight ageing of the population.

Finally, note the very general character of equation (8.5). Many populations in the broad sense of the term are not far from being stationary. Equation (8.5), linking the three basic parameters (annual number of arrivals in a population, average length of stay, population size), usefully enables us to specify the size of one parameter when we know the other two, e.g. (just one example) the average length of stay at school or university ($\overset{\circ}{e}_0$) when we know both the total size of the population (P) and the number of annual entrants (B). But, we repeat, the population in question must not be far from being stationary.

9 Problems
with diagrams
and calculations

The progress of a demographic study poses many practical
problems which often cause embarrassment and are often badly re-
solved. We have already looked at such problems as the construction
of population pyramids (section 2.2) and (very important) the
correct interpretation of different concepts of age. Here we shall
deal with some other questions that have not been discussed before.

9.1 Diagrams based on 'age'

Diagrams play a large part in the analysis and presentation of
results of a demographic study. They will often display a series of
frequencies for the series of ages to which the phenomenon in
question relates.

First, let us look at *rates* and take as an example the data in
Table 6.2. This deals with age-specific fertility rates and we shall
select those for Sweden (for 1905) and France (the 1931 birth cohort).
Let us examine a histogram for ages around 20 (see Fig. 9.1.1):

The Swedish rate at age 20 (70 per 1000) refers to the age
interval between birthdays 20 and 21.

The French rate at age 20 (101 per 1000) refers to the interval
between ages 19.5 and 20.5.

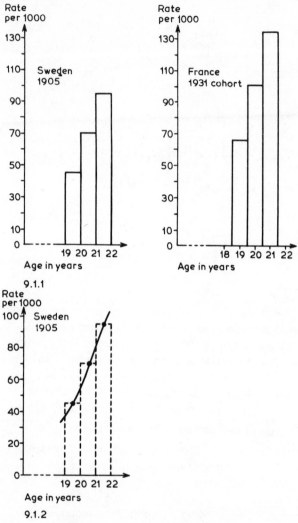

Fig. 9.1   Age-specific fertility rates

As a result, we associate with:

the Swedish rate, a rectangle of base extending from exact age 20 to exact age 21;

the French rate, a rectangle of base extending from age 19.5 to age 20.5.

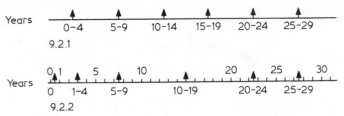

Fig. 9.2   Location of age groups in completed years

The different rectangles associated with the group of rates for a country (for year or for cohort) form the histogram representing this group. However, we usually prefer to substitute a continuous line (Fig. 9.1.2); thus, the middle points at the top of the rectangles are joined (the latter disappear) by a smooth line, which gives a less obtrusive effect and makes superimpositions more feasible (see, e.g., Figs 6.2 and 7.1). This is, of course, perfectly justifiable since there is continuous change in rates linked to continuously changing age.

Note as a corollary that this continuous line connecting rectangles (see Fig. 9.1.2) cannot take the place of a histogram for a phenomenon that is essentially discontinuous, e.g. the distribution of families by the number of children.

What has been said about rates also holds good for graphic representation of population characteristics varying with age, e.g. the proportion single (see Fig. 7.2, p. 100).

Lastly, what happens when rates refer to age groups of unequal extent? When extents *are* equal it is correct to locate the series of rates at equidistant points (Fig. 9.2.1). This we can no longer do when they are unequal and we must plot a scale of exact ages on which we shall locate the central ages of the groups in question. Thus, Fig. 9.2.2 shows the different widths along the scale corresponding to ages 0, 1–4, 5–9, 10–19, 20–24, and 25–29.

9.2   Semi-logarithmic paper

To illustrate certain phenomena with very rapid growth (with age, time, etc.) we use paper where the values on the ordinate are located according to their logarithms. Thus, the points

1, 2, 3, ..., 10, ..., 100

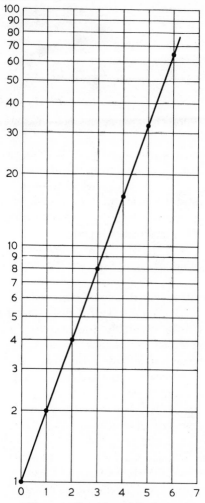

Fig. 9.3   Semi-logarithmic paper

will be located at the following proportional distances:

0;   0.301;   0.477;   ...;   1;   ...;   2.

Figure 9.3 gives an example of this type of paper, and Fig. 4.1, p. 40, shows the use made of it in representing changes in age-specific mortality rates.

With this type of scale on the ordinate, when the growth is

exponential (i.e. according to the principle of compound interest or geometric progression) the parameter is represented as a straight line. Thus, in Fig. 9.3 we have a series of values appearing in geometric progression:

1, 2, 4, 8, 16, 32, 64, ...

corresponding to a linear time flow:

0, 1, 2, 3, 4, 5, 6, ...

and the points are exactly aligned.

Thus, alignment on such paper shows exponential growth. The death rates and probabilities of dying above ages 25 or 30 are usually fairly well aligned and we sometimes, therefore, use semi-logarithmic paper in order to make adjustments and interpolations more easily.

9.3   Cartograms

Analysis of geographical variations in phenomena is an important part of comparative demography, which itself forms a basis for explanatory research.

This type of analysis very often appears in the form of carto-graphic illustrations which we therefore call *cartograms*. Here the geographical variations in an index are expressed by a range of colours or shadings which are then transferred to a map. The principles that must be followed can be seen from the example of the study of variations in the percentage of single men in the age group 50–54 in Great Britain at the 1971 census (see Table 9.1, Figs 9.4 and 9.5).

The essential question is the choice of media. Two alternatives are obvious:

we can resort to a larger or smaller variety of colours;
we can rely on systems of shading, stippling, hatching, etc., which allow a simple gradation from white to black through various shades of grey.

The former is really only for maps drawn by hand for special study (e.g. in a doctoral thesis; these maps are only exceptionally published as they are). We must resist the temptation to multiply

Table 9.1 Percentage of single men in the 50–54 age group in 1971, in the sub-regions of Great Britain

England and Wales

North

01	Industrial NE, North	10.6
02	Industrial NE, South	9.9
03	Rural NE, North	12.5
04	Rural NE, South	10.9
05	Cumberland and Westmorland	10.7

Yorkshire and Humberside

06	North Humberside	7.9
07	South Humberside	7.3
08	Mid Yorkshire	8.4
09	South Lindsey	9.2
10	South Yorkshire	7.9
11	Yorkshire coalfield	8.1
12	West Yorkshire	7.8

North West

13	South Cheshire (HP)	8.1
14	South Lancashire	8.5
15	Manchester	8.7
16	Merseyside	9.1
17	Furness	9.7
18	Fylde	6.7
19	Lancaster	8.3
20	Mid Lancashire	8.9
21	North East Lancashire	8.5

East Midlands

22	Notts. Derby coalfield and High Derbyshire	8.0
23	Nottingham, Derby	7.8
24	Leicester	7.2
25	Eastern lowlands	9.1
26	Northampton	7.4

West Midlands

27	Central (North)	7.5
28	Central (South)	7.6
29	Conurbation	8.8
30	Coventry belt	8.4
31	Rural West	10.0
32	North Staffordshire	7.8

East Anglia

33	South East	9.2
34	North East	8.0
35	North West	8.2
36	South West	8.6

South East

37	Greater London	10.8

Outer metropolitan area

38	West	6.9
39	North	6.7
40	East	5.6
41	South East	7.3
42	South	7.6
43	South West	6.3
44	Essex	8.1
45	Kent	7.1
46	Sussex coast	8.7
47	Solent	7.9
48	Beds and Bucks	7.8
49	Berks and Oxon	9.0

South West

50	Central	7.8
51	Southern	8.2
52	Western	7.9

Northern

53	North Gloucestershire	8.1
54	Bristol, Severnside	8.4
55	North Wiltshire	7.9

Wales

Industrial South Wales

56	Central and Eastern valleys	10.6
57	West South Wales	10.0
58	Coastal belt	8.9
59	North East Wales	8.5

North West Wales

60	North coast	8.3
61	Rest of North West Wales	12.7
62	Central Wales	16.6
63	South West Wales	12.2

Scotland

64	Highlands	16.9
65	North East	10.7
66	Tayside	10.3
67	Edinburgh	10.0
68	Falkirk/Stirling	10.9
69	Glasgow	10.9
70	South West	11.6
71	Borders	11.5

Fig. 9.4 Sub-regions of Great Britain

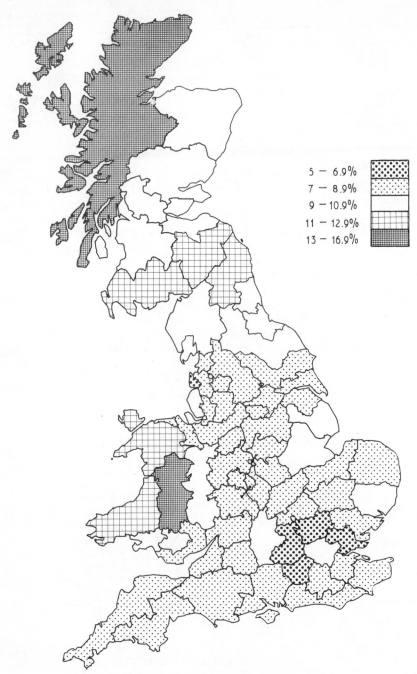

Fig. 9.5 Percentage of single men in the 50–54 age group

colours, and it is best to restrict ourselves to two and to indicate differences by variation in colour strength; thus, we can have a scale of blues (cold shades for regions with low index values) and a scale of reds (warm shades for high values), with white in the middle.[1] If the choice of colours is restricted in this way, we can immediately obtain a complete view of how the phenomenon in question varies by region, whereas if we have four, five or six colours to consider we shall constantly have to refer back to the key in order to interpret the map – and we shall never succeed in assimilating at a glance all the nuances offered to us.

However, the map – at least in published form – will usually be limited to a scale of grey extending from white to black. If we design skilfully, we can visually evoke the regions with lower index values (as blue did) by stippling more or less heavy or dense, and the regions with strong index values (as red did) by shading or hatching going up to black, with white always in the middle. This arrangement is obvious when we are dealing with values that are sometimes negative and sometimes positive, e.g. rates of increase in a population between two censuses (Fig. 9.6.)

Let us now make a cartogram from the data in Table 9.1. How should we decide on the percentage intervals the different tones will represent? The best way of doing this is to take an overall view of the phenomenon by constructing a histogram (Fig. 9.7). Having placed the values of the index (here the percentage single)[2] along the abscissa we stack the squares above each resulting segment, each square corresponding to a sub-region and being placed in the relevant percentage column; thus the sub-region of Cumberland and Westmorland (no. 05) with 10.7% single men is placed in the column for 10.0–10.9 inclusive.

We have, therefore, a distribution of conurbations and sub-divisions of the regions of England and Wales, and of the planning sub-regions of Scotland. For the central interval we choose the one that contains the median sub-region (no. 36 of 71). The choice of width of interval is linked to the need to have a reasonable total number of intervals (seven would seem to be the maximum); at either extremity we can have open-ended intervals

1 Of course, if the blue–white–red effect is not thought aesthetic (this will really only arise in the event of publication), we can always choose other colours.

2 With 71 sub-regions, there should not be more than about 16 index intervals so that the histogram may be adequately concentrated.

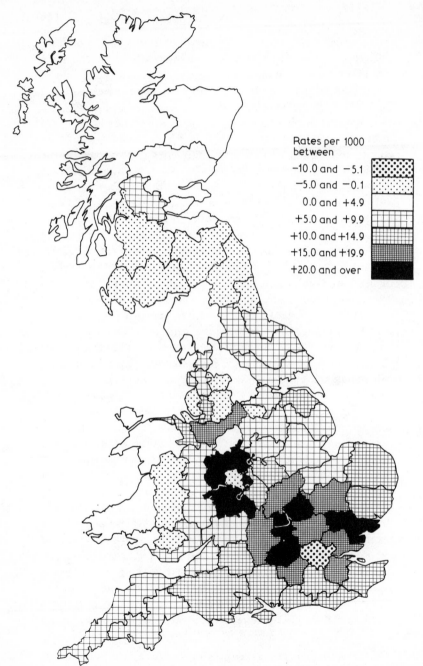

Rates per 1000
between

−10.0 and −5.1	
−5.0 and −0.1	
0.0 and +4.9	
+5.0 and +9.9	
+10.0 and +14.9	
+15.0 and +19.9	
+20.0 and over	

Fig. 9.6   Rates of population increase between 1961 and 1971

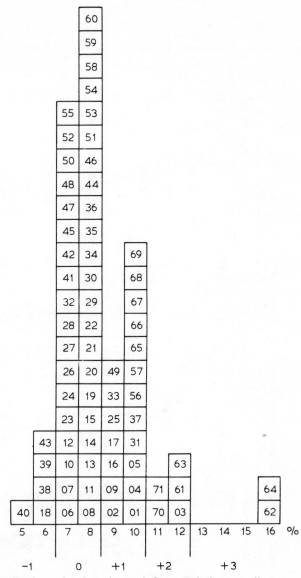

Fig. 9.7 Distribution of sub-regions of Great Britain according to percentage of single males in the 50–54 age group in 1971

Table 9.2 Distribution of births in England and Wales in 1971 where mother's age is 'not stated'

Mother's age (years)	Total births			Legitimate births			Illegitimate births		
	Real (1)	Distribution of 'not stated'* (2)	Corrected (3)	Real (4)	Distribution of 'not stated'* (5)	Corrected (6)	Real (7)	Distribution of 'not stated'* (8)	Corrected (9)
Less than 15	265	1	266	—	—	—	266	—	266
15	1245	3	1248	1	—	1	1244	3	1247
16	5832	15	5847	2900	8	2908	2931	8	2939
17	15421	41	15462	10149	27	10176	5272	14	5286
18	25653	68	25721	19721	52	19773	5932	16	5948
19	34007	90	34097	28154	74	28228	5853	15	5869
20	41904	111	42015	36573	97	36670	5331	14	5345
21	49341	131	49472	44539	118	44657	4802	13	4815
22	56291	149	56440	52069	138	52207	4222	11	4233
23	65452	173	63625	61442	162	61604	4010	11	4021
24	71961	190	72151	68341	181	68522	3619	10	3629
25	60158	159	60317	57174	151	57325	2984	8	2992
26	55851	148	55999	53283	141	53424	2568	7	2575
27	51329	136	51465	49095	130	49225	2234	6	2240
28	44226	117	44343	42210	111	42321	2017	5	2022
29	35022	93	35115	33318	88	33406	1704	5	1709
30	28914	76	28990	27413	72	27485	1501	4	1505
31	25407	67	25474	24046	64	24110	1360	4	1364

32	21614	57	21671	20355	54	20409	1259	3	1262
33	18203	48	18251	17079	45	17124	1124	3	1127
34	15190	40	15230	14201	37	14238	989	3	992
35	13041	35	13076	12199	32	12231	843	2	845
36	10738	28	10766	10015	26	10041	723	2	725
37	8684	23	8707	8085	21	8106	599	2	601
38	6956	18	6974	6438	17	6455	518	1	519
39	5686	15	5701	5226	14	5240	460	1	461
40	4550	12	4562	4172	11	4183	378	1	379
41	3184	8	3192	2904	8	2912	279	1	280
42	2085	6	2091	1893	5	1898	192	1	193
43	1310	4	1314	1170	3	1173	141	—	141
44	754	2	756	680	2	682	74	—	74
45	409	1	410	366	1	367	43	—	43
46	230	1	231	209	1	210	21	—	21
47	90	—	90	87	—	87	3	—	3
48	57	—	57	52	—	52	5	—	5
49	23	—	23	21	—	21	2	—	2
50 and over	6	—	6	6	—	6	—	—	—
Not stated	2066	—	—	1891	—	—	175	175	175
Total	783155	2066	783155	717477	1891	717477	65678	175	65678

[143]

* The totals are not distributed in the publications of the O.P.C.S. and are fictitiously provided here merely to demonstrate this particular method. In fact, births for which the mother's age is not stated are assigned the value of the appropriate item from the last case with otherwise similar characteristics to be processed.

without disadvantage, though the others should be of equal width.

In this way we are sure of producing a correctly differentiated view of the phenomenon. In our example, therefore, we shall distribute the tones according to the following scale of percentages: from 5.0 to 6.9; 7.0 to 8.9; 9.0 to 10.9; 11.0 to 12.9; and 13.0 and over.

9.4   Distribution of 'not stated' cases

This is a completely different problem that we very often have to solve.

When the data needed for basic demographic statistics are collected, some people do not give certain items of information required; these appear in tables under the heading 'not stated'. Thus, in a set of statistics of births distributed by the mother's age, there are some births where her age is not known. So as not to neglect these 'not stated' cases, which could be quite an important segment of the group (in this case 0.3%), we usually redistribute them in the way the persons for whom we have the information are distributed.

We can see in detail in Table 9.2 the calculations we must make. The births are given in column (1) and from a total of 783 155 there are 2066 where the mother's age was not stated. We shall rearrange the latter proportionately according to the distribution of the 781 089 (783 155 − 2066) for whom the information exists, by applying the fabtor:

$$\frac{2066}{781\,089} = 0.002645, \text{ or } 2.645 \text{ per } 1000$$

to the series 265, 1245, 5832, etc., of declared births.

This produces the figures in column (2), though in their gross form they give a total of 2064 instead of 2066, owing to rounding-off;[1] to make the total exact we alter the numbers for which this change entails the lowest relative error. Here the figure at age 35 has been raised to 35 (real value 34) and the figure at age 43 has been raised to 4 (real value 3). By adding the figures in columns (1) and (2) we obtain in column (3) data which include the 'not stated' cases.

1 Remember that rounding-off means retaining as the last digit the one that best approximates to the full number: i.e. 3.74 is rounded off to 3.7, 3.78 to 3.8, but 3.75 indifferently to either 3.7 or 3.8.

Since the 'not stated' cases occur among both legitimate and illegitimate births we can carry out the same operation for each. We arrive, therefore, at column (5) by multiplying the series in column (4) by 0.002643 (1891/715586 = 2.643 per 1000), and at column (8) by multiplying the series in column (7) by 0.002672 (175/65503 = 2.672 per 1000). By adding together columns (6) and (9) we obtain a series of corrected total births similar to column (3) which shows that the calculation of column (4) and subsequent columns was here unnecessary since the occurrence of 'not stated' cases is rather similar among both legitimate and illegitimate births.

At all events, this proportionality hypothesis is rather weak for this kind of distribution: it does not necessarily apply to the whole group in question but perhaps only to a segment of it; we do not always know.

In certain circumstances the hypothesis should be rejected, e.g. when the 'not stated' cases include people who believed that they were replying by not doing so; this might be the case with women who have had no live births and do not answer the question: how many live-born children have you had? It might also be true of parents whose child did not breathe at birth and who do not answer a question about erroneous stillbirth such as: did the child start to breathe?

There are more elaborate methods (e.g. for family sizes that are 'not stated') which enable us to make distributions that take into account this particular behaviour in one segment of the respondents.

Index